Communities
and Capital

Communities and Capital

Local Struggles against
Corporate Power and Privatization

*Edited by Thomas W. Collins
and John D. Wingard*

Southern Anthropological Society Proceedings, No. 33
Michael V. Angrosino, Series Editor

The University of Georgia Press
Athens and London

Southern Anthropological Society

Founded 1966

Published by the University of Georgia Press
Athens, Georgia 30602
© 2000 by the Southern Anthropological Society
All rights reserved
Set in 11/13 Times by Betty Palmer McDaniel
Printed and bound by McNaughton & Gunn, Inc.
The paper in this book meets the guidelines for
permanence and durability of the Committee on
Production Guidelines for Book Longevity of the
Council on Library Resources.

Printed in the United States of America
Library of Congress Cataloging-in-Publication Data
Communities and capital : local struggles against corporate power
    and privatization / edited by Thomas W. Collins and John D. Wingard.
        p. cm. — (Southern Anthropological Society proceedings ; no. 33)
    Includes bibliographical references and index.
    ISBN 0-8203-2172-9 (alk. paper)—
    ISBN 0-8203-2173-7 (pbk. : alk. paper)
    1. Economic anthropology. 2. Economic development. 3. Capitalism.
    4. International economic relations. 5. Economic policy. 6. Privatization.
    I. Collins, Thomas W. II. Wingard, John Davis, 1958– . III. Series.
    GN2.S9243   no. 33
    [GN448]
    306.3—dc21   99-29098

British Library Cataloging-in-Publication Data available

Contents

Communities
and Capital

Introduction

Thomas W. Collins

Capitalism, as Eric Wolf (1982) reminds us, has been around a long time, probably since before Columbus. It is a dynamic economic system that is accumulative and expansive. Once established, its tentacles spread and envelop peripheral societies both in industrial nations and in those at the margins. After four or five centuries of capitalism, there are no remote villages and no sources of labor that the system has not penetrated in some form. Perhaps this worldwide success has made *globalism* a more popular or precise concept than *capitalism* because it implies a new epoch of free trade, industrial restructuring, and greater ease of transfer of finance capital across international borders (Hirst and Thompson 1996; Tabb 1997). Popular writers such as Rifkin (1995) and Aronowitz and DiFazio (1994) view globalism as a qualitative change in the forces of production brought about by technology which, in turn, has led to major changes in social relations throughout the world. In the past two decades, corporations have certainly demonstrated an unprecedented ability to move capital around the world with little regard for national boundaries.

Goods and services are increasingly produced by a global assembly line in which phases of production occur in various locations in different countries. The new lean production described by Bennett Harrison (1994:150) abandons the vertical integration of the old assembly-line model ("Fordism") for a type of networked production over several regions, all managed by a just-in-time transportation delivery system. Labor capital has been downsized, retooled, and restructured to permit flexibility and diversity. New populations have been brought into this production system, which now reaches new sectors of workers that were more or less untouched before. In addition, industrial nations, in particular the United States, have promoted the creation of global economic institutions, like the World Trade Organization (WTO), the World Bank, and the International Monetary Fund (IMF), and regional ones, like the European Union (EU) and North American Free Trade Agreement (NAFTA). These agencies assist and protect corporate expansion. For example, the past two sessions of the U.S. Congress have featured extensive debate over "fast-track legislation," which would permit the administration to negotiate additional trade treaties while limiting debate from various interest groups concerned with labor and environmental issues. The concept of globalism has been pervasive and powerful, at least until the collapse of Asian economies in 1998; most politicians from the moderate left to the far right have therefore accepted the corporate view that there is no alternative.

Whether this is a new era or just a more mature type of capitalism is not critical for our purposes in this volume. The point is that a worldwide market system is a force with which every community must contend and negotiate and against which it must at times struggle. As we will see in the following chapters, the benefits are not always balanced. There is a great deal of social injustice. Corporations are still bent on extracting more value from labor. Communities, however, may become the new sources of strength, replacing the old class conflicts and international labor organizations. In so doing they have the potential to become a countervailing force in this global system.

The nine papers in this volume represent a variety of experiences with global capitalism at the community or regional levels. Many of the contributors have conceptualized globalism in a manner that is unique to their particular region or degree of involvement in the production system. In every case, however, globalism has impacted the traditions and established social relationships. Privatization of the commons or community-owned resources (Wingard, Garrity-Blake) proposed in the name of greater economic efficiency threatens to restrict public access to vital resources. Grassroots development (Bort and Sabella) and local use of resources (Kedia), strategies that were initially environmentally friendly and that still turn a profit, are pushed aside and abandoned as large capital interests enter the market. Monopoly control of markets disempowers both basic producers and labor (Moberg), leaving them with little recourse other than to accept extremely low product prices and wages. Demand for flexible, easily manipulated labor (Grey) creates demands for international migration at a level not seen in the United States since the late nineteenth century. Regional trade treaties such as NAFTA have eliminated jobs held for decades (Skipper), depriving industrial workers of the security of pensions earned through a lifetime of productive, profit-generating labor. Privatization and downsizing in the public sector have reversed the political and economic gains that African American laborers achieved a generation ago through the struggles of the civil rights movement of the 1960s. Government projects and services that generated public sector employment for minorities in the 1970s are underfunded or have been privatized. Privatized jobs are parceled out through rings of subcontractors; such jobs are generally nonunion and pay relatively low wages. People who rely on these jobs, such as public housing residents in Memphis (Spangler), are pushed into the irregular economy. At the same time, privatization in the name of economic efficiency (S. Collins) threatens to deprive poor and working-class people of basic, publicly provided services essential to fill the gaps left by low wages and unemployment.

It is still too early to predict the long-term economic and social consequences of the current recessions in Russia and Asia, although it is evident that the pace of globalization will be slowed. Whether its course will be changed, however, remains to be seen. It is nonetheless apparent that despite the popular rhetoric supporting the "New World Order," there is a growing sense that something is fundamentally wrong, both with a system that treats people as mere inputs in a productive process and with the scholarly models generated to explain and support that system. Socialism may have failed as an alternative, but it is premature to say that there is *no* alternative. The alternative, as suggested by the papers in this volume, may be in the very communities most impacted by the effects of globalism and the neoclassical economic rationale that supports it.

Our role as anthropologists and social economists may be to document these incipient alternatives, communicate them to the wider public, and encourage them to coalesce into a viable response to the current dominant paradigm. What can we expect in terms of a grassroots revitalization movement as we enter the twenty-first century? What forms or new structures must evolve to transform the community into a viable and effective force within the social relationships generated by globalism? The papers in this volume can be viewed as a beginning of the crucial process of addressing these questions.

REFERENCES

Aronowitz, S., and W. DiFazio. 1994. *The Jobless Future*. Minneapolis: University of Minnesota Press.

Harrison, B. 1994. *Lean and Mean: The Changing Landscape of Corporate Power in the Age of Flexibility*. New York: Basic Books.

Hirst, P., and G. Thompson. 1996. *Globalization in Question*. Cambridge: Polity Press.

Rifkin, J. 1995. *The End of Work*. New York: G. P. Putnam's Sons.

Tabb, W. K. 1997. Globalization Is *an* Issue, the Power of Capital Is *the* Issue. *Monthly Review* 49(2):20–30.

Wolf, E. 1982. *Europe and the People without History*. Berkeley: University of California Press.

Finding Alternatives to Privatizing the Resource: Community-Focused Management for Marine Fisheries

John D. Wingard

The collapse of communism in most parts of the world has left capitalism in the virtually unchallenged position of paramount organizing principle, with neoclassical economics its dominant theoretical paradigm. Popular political rhetoric espouses the power of competition. The free market is seen as the answer to global problems. National borders are regarded as obstructions to the free flow of goods and capital (though essential to control the flow of people). These views are reiterated and reinforced by high-profile economists, talk show pundits, and mainstream journalists. And because no viable alternatives seem apparent, this model structures the production and consumption of everything from computer chips manufactured in Silicon Valley to fish captured on the high seas.

In this essay I will briefly explore why the current version of capitalism has become so widely accepted. I will also give a short overview of the recent history of the U.S. fishing industry, followed by an examination of the current reliance on neoclassical economic models in the area of fishery management. I will then discuss alternative approaches to fishery management that are more appropriate than those currently advocated by neoclassical economists.

THE HEGEMONY OF THE NEOCLASSICAL PARADIGM

Why has the neoclassical paradigm been so widely accepted? The most obvious answer to this question is that, in many circumstances, the neoclassical model has been extremely successful. One cannot deny that huge amounts of wealth have been created under this system of production. One cannot deny the large number of innovations that have been spawned within this system. And finally, one cannot deny that more people are living more secure lives at a higher level of material well-being than at any time in human history. And it is these success stories that advocates of the paradigm like to hold up as their proof of the efficacy of the system.

Of course, there is also a flip side to each of these points. The wealth that has been created is concentrated in the hands of a small minority of the world's population. The innovations have likewise benefited only a small minority. Despite tremendous advances in food production, communication, and medical science, vast numbers of the world's people remain malnourished, illiterate, and without access to health care. And finally, the number of people living in absolute poverty (more than one out of every four persons in Third World countries) currently exceeds the total world population of a little over a century ago (UNDP 1994).

A second factor that has contributed significantly to the success of the neoclassical model of capitalism has been its ability to align itself with principles derived from the natural sciences. In the twentieth century, the discipline of economics has made a conscious decision to model itself after physics (Daly and Cobb 1994:30). This alliance has imbued economics with a certain "natural" quality. The implication is that just as physicists are attempting to discover natural laws about the physical world, economists are attempting to discover natural laws about human behavior. The neoclassical paradigm has therefore embedded itself in our worldview by aligning itself with our perceptions of the "real world." It is no coincidence that neoclassical economics still embodies a large, though frequently denied, degree of economic if not social Darwinism.

Economics, however, differs in a fundamental way from physics. Physicists must always evaluate their theories against a natural world, one over which they have little power—i.e., natural, largely immutable *laws* can be said to exist. To the extent that scientific theories do not conform to or agree with these laws, the physicists' theories will inevitably have to be altered. Economists, on the other hand, do not have this ultimate standard against which to measure their theories. Human societies are almost infinitely plastic. Thurow (1984:21) has pointed out that when an economic theory does not conform to the observed world, economists, unlike their counterparts in physics, *can alter the observed world (society) to conform to their theory.* In fact, economists spend a great deal of time developing policies that have the intent of "managing" human behavior so as to bring it into line with the theories they have generated.

In addition, many economists assert that, like physical science, theirs is an objective, value-free science (Koch 1976:9). This goal, however, may not be attainable. As Brockway (1995:38–39) puts it, "The vocabulary of physics is amoral—not antimoral, but amoral." The variables studied by physicists have no moral implications because the laws describing them have no alternatives. The vocabulary of economics, in contrast, abounds in ethical terms. It is impossible to define "good," "service," or even "utility" without making ethical judgments.

Another implication of modeling economics after physics is an almost exclusive reliance on mathematical models which, in turn, rely on quantifiable data. If it cannot be quantified, it is difficult to model and is ultimately discounted or largely ignored. Other social scientists, such as anthropologists, are acutely aware of how much of human behavior defies quantification. An example of this tendency is the economists' treatment of value. In a recent predraft fishery management plan, the "true value" of a fishery is defined as net economic benefit, which in turn is defined as the difference between producer surplus (producer revenues minus production costs) and consumer surplus (willingness to pay minus purchase price). Note that all of these measures rely almost exclusively on monetary valuations derived from market transactions. Nowhere is there any mention of nonfinancial attributes, such as the value of fishers' human and social capital that is used (and wasted when not used). An economist might argue that human and social capital are indirectly accounted for in such measures as production costs, but it is, at best, a partial accounting.

Another limitation of reliance on mathematical models is that human behavior is motivated by multiple factors. Interlocking patterns of shifting and fluctuating motives may be operative in any social setting. To capture these patterns in a mathematical model is impossible (Harré, Clark, and de Carlo 1985). Economists have dealt with this problem by grossly simplifying human behavior, thus drastically reducing the explanatory power of their models.

A final implication of modeling economics after physics is that the "laws" discovered are perceived as nomothetic, that is, they can be applied to any situation where economic activity occurs. Just as a physicist assumes that the same physical laws that operate on earth also operate in the Andromeda galaxy, economists have come to assume that economic models that work on the floor of the stock exchange should work on the deck of a fishing boat. Fishermen may seem to act unnaturally in depleting the world's fishery resources and irrationally when called upon to alter their behavior. To explain these problems, economists turn to their usual theories, which may not really be relevant to the conditions of fisheries around the world.

THE CHANGING FISHING INDUSTRY

In the past twenty years, many industries in the United States, including the fishing industry, have experienced downsizing and other changes of status. These changes have had dramatic impacts on fishermen, their families, and their communities. Expansion of the fleet, the addition of new technology, and global competition have resulted in new management challenges for all fisheries. Government measures to promote healthy fishing stocks have, among other things, closed fisheries, minimized days at sea, limited access, and closed areas to fishing. Traditional methods of harvesting once free and abundant natural resources have changed. Fishermen, their families, and their communities, along with resource managers, are facing difficult choices.

Shortly after the Second World War, the federal government began an ongoing effort to aid the fishing industry.[1] Its assistance policies have attempted to deal with a changing cast of villains, which has included cheap foreign labor, subsidization of fishing fleets in other nations, inadequate domestic demand for fish products, and inadequate and flawed science. Policies, admittedly misguided and ill conceived in many, if not most, cases, have relied on the raising of tariffs on fish products, the promotion of domestic consumption of fish products, the creation of programs to increase the competitive position of the domestic fleet, the establishment of an Exclusive Economic Zone and exclusion of foreign vessels from that zone, and the development of vessel buyback programs to reduce pressure on the resource (Dewar 1983).

In addition to these direct efforts, fishermen have also reaped indirect benefits as well, especially in the area of technology. For example, fishermen benefited from decades of taxpayer-funded cold war defense industry research in underwater submarine surveillance and open-water location tracking technology. The LORAN and satellite-based geographical positioning systems, for example, enable captains to mark and record their positions with unprecedented accuracy. Echo sounders developed for submarine warfare provide the means of finding schools of fish, locating shipwrecks where fish collect, and avoiding obstacles that can damage gear. The industry also benefited from advances in underwater mapping of the ocean floor. Other significant inventions include onboard refrigeration, durable nylon and synthetic fiber for nets, and seaplanes and helicopters to locate schools of fish. The federal government also has directly sponsored much marketing research through funds provided under the Dingell-Johnson Act of 1950 and Wallop-Breaux Amendments, the Saltonstall-Kennedy Act of 1954, and the Commercial Fisheries Research and Development Act of 1964 (USDOC 1996:17).

Several government-sponsored fleet subsidization efforts accompanied the development of new technology. The 1964 amendment to the Fishing Fleet Improvement Act financed up to 50 percent of vessel construction costs. The 1970 Fishing Vessel Construction Fund Program deferred payment of federal income taxes provided that the money was used to construct or reconstruct a vessel. The 1973 Fishing Fleet Vessel Obligation Guarantee Program financed up to 87.5 percent of the cost of construction, reconstruction, or reconditioning of fishing vessels and shoreside facilities (USDOC 1996:16–17).

The combination of new technology and financial incentives encouraged the entrance of many newcomers to the industry, some of whom were relatively unskilled weekend fishermen. It was believed by some that what this new group of fishermen lacked in old-fashioned grit and "sea smarts," they could make up for with cutting-edge technology. Seasoned skippers similarly upgraded their investments with larger boats, greater horsepower, and new technology. Their used boats were made available to new fishermen who wished to partake of the new prosperity. The number of U.S. commercial fishing vessels increased from around 12,000 in 1966 to nearly 17,000 in 1976 and then to about 23,000 in 1987. These numbers show the evolution of the U.S. fleet in absolute numbers, but they do not reveal the enormous gains in fishing power afforded by technology and ingenuity (USDOC 1996:16).

The investments initially paid off. Between 1974 and 1993, U.S. commercial landings increased from less than 2 million metric tons to nearly 5 million metric tons. But the harvest pressure on the stocks was exceeding their capacity to replace themselves, a problem exemplified by declining sizes (i.e., younger fish were being caught before they could reach maturity), declining catch per unit effort (an indicator of availability), and declining values (an indication that fishermen were shifting to lower valued species as more favored species declined) (USDOC 1996:17–18). But as the fish stocks dropped off, the fishermen intensified their effort, with increased trips and more days at sea. Continuing the competitive treadmill, boats kept adding new technology.

As the fisheries' resources diminished, new management strategies and regulations were called into play. As a first step, the United States declared that waters 200 miles out from its shores formed an Exclusive Economic Zone (EEZ). This policy allowed the United States to exclude foreign vessels from fishing in these waters. The prevailing belief was that foreign vessels, especially large Soviet trawlers, were "vacuuming" the seas (Dewar 1983).

In conjunction with this move, Congress passed the Fisheries Conservation and Management Act (FCMA), known in later renditions as the Magnuson Act and most recently as the Magnuson-Stevens Act. The FCMA went into effect January 1, 1977. Acting under the authority of the FCMA, eight regional fishery management councils were established.[2] These councils eventually included representatives from industry, state and federal governments, recreational fishing interests, and environmental groups. The responsibility of the councils was to establish fishing regulations that would result in the optimum sustainable yields for each fishery. In establishing optimal sustainable yield (OSY), the councils were to consider biological, economic, and social inputs.

The void left by the exclusion of foreign fleets was quickly filled by domestic vessels. The ability of the councils to manage the EEZ fisheries in an effective manner proved to be exceedingly limited (Dewar 1983). Problems have arisen over determining, monitoring, and maintaining viable levels of economically important fish populations. It has been difficult for the councils to respond to pressures from conflicting fishing interests and their representatives. There were also enforcement and equity issues that engulfed the councils soon after their establishment and that continue to be problematic even today.

After over two decades of federal management efforts, overfishing continues to be a major problem, and the industry is severely overcapitalized; there are too many boats chasing too few fish. An assessment of fish stocks showed that as of the years 1992–94, 44 percent of 157 known stock groups were being fully utilized, or harvested at levels just equal to the long-term sustainable yield level. Another 36 percent were being overutilized, or harvested at levels exceeding long-term sustainable yield levels. In other words, 80 percent of known stocks are being harvested at the margin of or beyond sustainable yields (USDOC 1995).

FISHERY MANAGEMENT STRATEGIES

That world fishery stocks are severely overfished and depleted is well known not only within industry and environmental circles but by the general public, as demonstrated by the recent decision of several prominent restaurants to place a moratorium on serving swordfish (Hallowell 1998; Conover 1998). Swordfish, however, is only one of literally hundreds of fish species that are threatened with economic extinction worldwide (McGoodwin 1991; Weber 1994; McQuaid 1996).

Current Management Strategies

Management efforts under the FCMA have attempted through various measures to reduce harvesting pressures on the fish stocks. Several management strategies have been employed, including operational controls, effort controls, and catch controls. These strategies are usually used in combination.

Operational controls focus on how the fishery operates and only indirectly on factors causing fish mortality. The methods employed either selectively or generally reduce the vulnerability of the stocks. Methods include restrictions on the types of gear used, closure of particular locations such as spawning and aggregation areas, and restrictions on the retention of fish meeting certain criteria (usually size restrictions). Effort controls focus directly on factors affecting fish mortality. Methods include vessel control (limiting the number and/or size of vessels) and time controls (limiting the number of days or parts of the year permitted for fishing). Effort controls restrict flexibility on the part of fishermen and limit participation. Catch controls typically employ a quota on the landings of a particular species. Quotas can be geared toward either achieving a desired harvest rate consistent with the long-term productivity of the species or achieving a desired stock level over time.

Each of these approaches has a number of drawbacks from a management perspective. For example, operational controls can be very difficult to enforce, particularly where fishermen are permitted to target more than one type of fish using different gear types but are not able to use all gear types on all the targeted fish. Retention restrictions often lead to very wasteful bycatch problems. Fish pulled up from deep water are usually dead or damaged by the time they are landed on the vessel. Even if they are thrown back, they frequently do not survive. Moreover, since many fish stocks mix with other stocks, restrictions placed on one stock may make it difficult or impossible to fish a stock that has no restrictions. Vessel controls are frequently resented by fishermen who are excluded from a fishery they may have utilized in the past. Vessel controls also make it difficult to switch from one fishery to another as conditions change. Rules determining who is given access are often seen as capricious at best and deliberately biased at worst. Time controls often lead to "derby fishing," when there is a mad rush to capture as many fish as possible in the short period of time allotted (hours in some extreme cases). This policy can lead fishermen to adopt unsafe fishing practices. If the open times happen to occur during periods of bad weather, fishermen are forced to take additional risks in an already risky venture in order to catch the fish. Catch controls have been problematic because the scientific knowledge about many key fish species is incomplete and inconclusive. It is extremely difficult to define target population levels or harvest rates with an adequate degree of certainty. If population levels are set too low or harvest rates too high, the fish stock may continue to decline even if all other regulations are enforced. On the other hand, if population levels are too high or harvest levels too low, fishermen suffer unnecessary economic hardships, particularly when dealing with highly migratory fish stocks like tuna that are harvested on an international basis. Domestic fishermen feel they are unfairly penalized when their catch levels are restricted, since the fish they avoid are merely captured by fishermen from other nations. And finally, these management strategies are only as effective as the enforcement efforts applied to them. With the large number of boats, multitude of regulations, and vast areas of open ocean to be monitored, noncompliance is a major problem.

Neoclassical Management Strategies

For decades, quotas have gotten smaller, fishing times have gotten shorter, and the list of allowable gear has shrunk. Meanwhile, fish stocks continue to decline. Management has increasingly focused on the question of open access. Most managers feel that until access to the fish is greatly reduced, there will be problems of overcapitalization, overfishing, and ineffective management.

Defenders of open access often romanticize the seas as a last frontier. In many communities, the sea is an employer of last resort during periods of economic downturn in other sectors. To some, open access is a reflection of the American ethic of social equality. And to others, it is an embodiment of laissez-faire competition (McCay 1987). There is little dispute, however, among those most familiar with the current situation that open access is not a viable option. The resources are severely over-utilized, and there is a very real danger that many economically important resources may be destroyed beyond recovery, thus depriving future generations of their benefit and potentially causing extensive changes in the marine ecosystem (Pauley et al. 1998).

The prevailing models being considered for limiting access are firmly rooted in the tenets of neoclassical economic theory and its focus on economic efficiency. Economists point to resources being wasted in the overcapitalized, overexploited fishing industry. They argue that society benefits when resources are utilized in the most efficient (usually defined as profitable) way. In particular, there has been an attempt to limit access by creating some form of property rights (or privileges). Property rights are viewed as the best way to achieve the most efficient use of resources.

Property rights, particularly those referring to private property, are an integral component of the neoclassical model, according to which such rights guarantee that the benefits of investment will be reaped by the investor. Since the owner of the property can be guaranteed any proceeds generated by the use of the property, the incentive will be to utilize the resource in an efficient, sustainable way.

Individual Transferable Quotas

The most widely discussed form of property rights involves the issuing of Individual Transferable Quotas (ITQs), which most closely emulate true property rights. In its purer forms, this approach envisions a fishery exploited by a small number of highly capitalized boats, each with a definable property right in that fishery. Fewer boats means less fishing effort, fewer management problems, and greater enforceability.

An ITQ is an allocated privilege of landing a specified portion of the total annual fish catch in the form of quota shares, which designate how the total annual fish catch (i.e., the total allowable catch, or TAC) is to be subdivided into specified portions for individual quota holders. ITQ shares are transferable; holders of shares can buy, sell, or lease them depending on how much they elect to participate in the fishery. ITQ programs are intended to reduce overcapitalization, promote conservation of stocks, improve market conditions, promote safety in the fishing fleet, enhance enforceability, foster employment and community stability, create wealth, and promote equity (Buck 1995).[3]

ITQ programs will reduce overcapitalization by limiting the number of fishermen/vessels that hold quota shares. Because competition will be greatly reduced, fishermen will no longer have to invest in new technology to stay competitive. And because the fishing will be spread out over a longer season, fishermen may actually be able to reduce the size and power of their boats.

Stock conservation will result from the vested interest in sustainability that derives from ownership. Because quota holders no longer operate under the philosophy of "What I don't catch, somebody else will," they will be more inclined to fish more carefully and perhaps forego fishing if holding off will yield market or other benefits. Since the fishermen have long-term predictable access to the fishery, the long-term health of the stock is of much greater concern to them.

Market conditions will improve for several reasons. First, under the current open access regime, fishermen feel compelled to catch as many fish as quickly as possible before someone else gets them, resulting in both a glut of fish arriving on the market at the same time and a very short period of availability as the quota is filled rapidly. This policy also puts a premium on quantity rather than quality. Under an ITQ system, fishermen can time their fishing effort to respond to market conditions. If the supply of fish becomes too large and prices drop, fishermen will be able to wait for better prices, knowing the fish will still be there. Moreover, because there is no rush to fish, fishermen will be able to fish more carefully and increase the quality of fish caught. Safety will be improved because fishermen will have more discretion over when to fish. They will no longer be compelled to go to sea in unfavorable conditions to secure a share of the catch. As the pace of fishing slows, the accident rate will decrease.

ITQs are expected to enhance enforceability in several ways. First, because there will be fewer boats, it will be easier to monitor their activities. Some have even proposed that a federal observer on board could be a requirement for quota holders. Second, because each fisherman's quota will have to be monitored closely, the ability to cheat will be reduced.

Third, disincentives to cheat will also derive from the inherent sustainability of incentives resulting from ownership. And finally, the threat of losing one's quota for violations would serve as a powerful deterrent to cheating. Employment and community stability are expected to improve as well. Under an ITQ program, jobs in the fishing industry are anticipated to become more stable and permanent, replacing the short, temporary, or seasonal jobs characteristic of many open access fisheries.

Overcapitalization is almost as problematic as overfishing. Too much wealth is devoted to the fishing industry. By one estimate, it cost $92 billion to capture $70 billion worth of fish on a worldwide basis in 1989 (FAO 1993). A U.S. example is the New England Multispecies Groundfish Fishery (MGF), one of the most severely stressed large commercial fisheries. The economic benefits in the MGF could be increased $150 million annually, but would require a 70 percent reduction in effort (Edwards and Murawski 1993). Economists argue that direct economic losses result from capital invested in the fishing industry that could be better utilized in other sectors of the economy. Indirect losses are incurred by the lower value of the marine resources harvested under an open access regime.

Through their reliance on the markets, ITQs offer a way to solve these problems, and they are a key component of the neoclassical argument to the extent that reliance on market forces will drive the advantages of an ITQ system. In their strongest form, ITQs can be bought, sold, traded, and rented. The most efficient fishers and those who can add the most value to their catch become more of a force. In a fishery based on property rights, the stronger will buy out the weaker (Crowley 1996). The capital left in the industry will be better used elsewhere. Advocates also argue that social equity will be improved as fishermen wishing to enter the fishery will be able to purchase secure quota shares without having to wage an expensive battle for share, as they must do under the open access policy.

In summary, according to ITQ proponents, the benefits deriving from the system will be realized through the rationalizing powers of the free market. Shares will go to the producers with the lowest costs, who are thereby considered the most efficient. Inefficient fishermen will be driven from the market. Share prices will reflect the true value of the resource. Excess capital and labor will be reallocated elsewhere in the economy. And the fish stocks will be harvested at sustainable levels.

ALTERNATIVE MANAGEMENT STRATEGIES

The ITQ model advocated by neoclassical economists clearly has a number of significant merits. Parts of it, however, are based on assumptions that may not be appropriate for the management of either fish or fishermen. This is not to say that ITQs should be ignored, but it is important to consider that how ITQs are implemented and used can have profound effects on fishermen, communities, and natural resources. There are alternative management strategies that more closely correspond to the realities of the fishing industry. These strategies rely less on efficiency-oriented market principles than on equity-oriented community principles.

Economists could, at least in theory, model the outcome of a purely market-driven ITQ system, but the outcome of a community approach will be highly variable. Rather than impersonal market forces guiding the decision-making process, people in communities will be making the decisions. The outcomes, therefore, will be as different as the communities—and "community" itself is a concept that may be defined in various ways. The central theme of a community approach is to optimize along a number of dimensions, of which flexibility, equity, and sustainability of the long-term productivity of the resource are the most important. This optimization will not represent an absolute point, such as might be achieved from an economic model, but will be the result of interaction and negotiation among members of a bounded community; even the boundaries of the community may be negotiable, at least initially. The outcome of such a system may not be easily predicted, but it will be more realistic.

Marine resource management, with fisheries being a major component, involves a number of interlinked issues, including (1) form and determination of access; (2) the social and economic costs of worker (fisher) displacement; (3) fishing as one component of a multicomponent income strategy; (4) the economic pursuit of quality; and (5) the implications for biological management of different forms of property rights. Neoclassical management schemes tend to emphasize a subset of these issues with others receiving much less attention. Comprehensive, sustainable management, however, requires that all of these issues be addressed in a comprehensive manner recognizing the interrelationships and interlinkages among them. A community approach to management has the potential for flexibility and inclusiveness necessary to achieve this comprehensiveness.

Form and Determination of Access

As discussed above, current management efforts are increasingly addressing the negative impacts of open access. In terms of access to the resource, one can conceptualize a continuum, one end representing pure open access (i.e., anybody who wants to can capture the resource) and the other end representing limitations to one individual or firm. Neither of these extremes currently exists, nor are they likely to exist in the future. On the open access end, there are a number of barriers to entry, including cost of technology, skills, and geographic access. On the other end, it is unlikely that monopolistic access would ever be a politically acceptable solution to the problem. The debate, however, has tended to gravitate toward one pole or the other.

MARKET APPROACH

While monopolistic access may be deemed unacceptable, oligopolistic access is seen to be a viable, even preferable model by many managers. This scenario involves a few highly capitalized boats manned by full-time fishermen working the fishery. ITQ systems are seen as a mechanism to achieve this structure, with the market for ITQs determining the final number and configuration of participants. Quota shares will be bid up by the market to the point where they reflect the true value of the fishery. Efficient, well capitalized fishermen will purchase the quotas at the market price. Inefficient fishermen will either sell their quotas (assuming they received initial allocations) or will not be able to purchase any at the market-determined price. These latter fishermen, along with their boats, will represent part of the inefficient labor and capital squeezed out of the system. More labor and capital will be removed as the remaining fishermen will be better able to match their capital investments and labor use with the amount needed to harvest their quota shares. As a result, there will be further reductions in capital as inefficient boats are replaced with more efficient ones. Likewise, unneeded labor will be let go.

In summary, the problem of overcapitalization will have been efficiently resolved. The fishery will be utilized by the most efficient fishermen using the most efficient technology. The displaced capital will be available to be used more efficiently elsewhere by society. The fear of opponents of market-determined ITQ access is that quotas will become highly concentrated in the hands of a few. Rather than rewarding the most efficient fishermen, distribution of quota shares may better reflect the distribution of capital. Operators with access to capital, including corporate investors, will be best positioned to get quota share (Buck 1995). Those fishermen hired back by corporate investors will find themselves in radically different and largely undesirable working relationships—more like factory jobs than the highly independent, self-reliant positions they formerly filled (Griffith and Dyer 1996:6). Concentration could also lead to less competition and higher consumer prices, as so often happens under an oligopolistic system.

COMMUNITY APPROACH

A community approach to management will be more centrally located along the open access/market-determined continuum. Fish are a highly unpredictable resource. Fish populations vary, often unpredictably, along a number of dimensions. There is year-to-year fluctuation in population levels. There is variation in their geographic locations from one year to the next (or even from one part of the year to the next). Moreover, weather and water conditions add to the uncertainties confronting the fishermen. On the economic side, market prices for fish vary in response to a number of factors beyond immediate supply. The size and value of quota shares will therefore vary greatly from one year to the next.

The fishing industry under a purely market-driven ITQ system will consist of a small number of highly capitalized boats, each requiring a relatively large absolute quantity of fish to remain economically viable. In years of low fish stocks, there will be significant pressure brought to bear on resource managers to keep the quota levels high enough to maintain the economic viability of these fishermen. The composition of the fishing industry under a market-determined structure may differ in terms of political power as well. The fishing industry may come to be dominated by corporations, which are more likely than small-scale producers to have political clout and which, through their size and organization, can apply extra pressure on managers.

A community-focused management approach will consist of less capitalized part-time fishermen[4] who can afford to be flexible in responding to annual fluctuations in fish stocks. As only a part of their income derives from fishing or from fishing a particular stock, the need to keep quota levels high will be lessened. In particular, fishermen at the lower margin may forego fishing completely, thus contributing to increased prices for those who do fish and also promoting the recovery of the stocks.

A management body, rather than the market, will determine the operation and configuration of the fishery. This responsibility should be distributed as widely as possible down to the level of individual coastal communities. One scenario could be that overall quotas be set by the National Marine Fisheries Service, with allocations then delegated to the currently existing Fishery Management Councils, which would further devolve the responsibility, possibly through states, to the community level. Models for such arrangements already exist in Canada (CCN 1997). Allocations are then determined by community boards that consist of various interest groups including fishermen, processors, shore-based workers, elected officials, and natural and social scientists. This procedure would allow communities to determine the best allocation of quotas based on a wide range of community issues besides strict economic efficiency as defined by economic models.

Social and Economic Costs of Worker (Fisher) Displacement

It is widely recognized that there is currently more capital and labor devoted to fishing than is needed to harvest the resource efficiently. Advocates of market-based ITQs see them as an effective way to eliminate this excess labor and capital. Once removed from the fishing industry, these resources can be better used elsewhere in the economy.

MARKET APPROACH

This argument rests on two assumptions that are violated in many segments of the fishing industry: factor mobility and alternative uses of displaced labor. Economists rightly point out the costs to society of an inefficient use of inputs, including labor. In order for the labor removed from the fishery to be used elsewhere in the economy, economic theory assumes that the units of labor (people) will go where there are other jobs. The reality of the situation is that people hold many roles in life beyond those associated with employment. For example, people involved in fishing frequently have strong ties to their communities that extend beyond their participation in fishing as an occupation. They have large extended families in the communities where they live, and/or multigenerational ties to the area. These people are therefore often reluctant to leave the fishery and move to distant communities to find work. This concern, in and of itself, has provided a strong incentive for many to remain in fishing well after rational economic analysis would suggest otherwise.

The second assumption concerns alternative employment opportunities, particularly employment that uses the displaced labor more efficiently than does the fishery. It is highly questionable if in fact such opportunities exist for many of the people most likely to be displaced, particularly fishing boat crews (Griffith and Dyer 1996:6).

If the result of displacement is increased costs to society in the form of government support in one form or another, the benefits to society are greatly reduced and may, in fact, yield a net loss. Management plans that result in a small number of full-time fishermen will require the displacement of a large number of people who currently derive at least a portion of their income from fishing. The government has already spent millions of dollars on worker retraining programs. There are also unaccounted expenses, including increased social costs that frequently accompany the displacement of workers, such as increased rates of alcoholism, increased incidents of spouse and child abuse, and physical and psychological disorders (Betts 1997; Binkley 1997). These costs are rarely, if ever, entered into the economic models used to evaluate various management options. If they were, the cost-benefit analyses might yield substantially different results.

COMMUNITY APPROACH

Under a community approach to management, a large number of people will be able to remain in the fishery on at least a part-time basis. In addition, because those most familiar with local conditions will be making the ultimate allocation decisions, access to resources (both fishing and nonfishing) can be optimized to minimize hardships, thus greatly reducing the social and economic costs associated with displacement.

Fishing as One Component of a Multicomponent Income Strategy

Under a market approach, the tendency will be to end up with a minimal number of full-time fishermen, even though reducing the number of people with access to the fishery may not be the most appropriate strategy given the direction in which the labor market is moving. Prior to the industrialization of fishing, the majority of fishermen were part-timers. Fishing was done on a seasonal or intermittent basis and was undertaken in tandem with other types of work.

MARKET APPROACH

This model of a multicomponent income strategy continues today (Griffith and Dyer 1996:6) and may become more common given transformations in the labor market. For the past two decades, employment arrangements in the United States have been changing. In the past, the typical career paradigm was characterized by lifetime employment with a single employer, steady advance up the job ladder, and a pension upon retirement. But this pattern is becoming less common as Nonstandard Work Arrangements (NSWAs) come to the fore (EPI 1997).

NSWAs include independent contracting, working for a temporary help agency, contract and on-call work, day labor, self-employment, and regular part-time employment. In 1995, 29.4 percent of all jobs were in NSWAs, with 34.5 percent of females and 25.3 percent of males so employed. Many fishermen are already employed in NSWAs, with fishing being the central component, even if it is not always the main income generator. When alternative jobs are taken, they mainly help fishermen weather the storm, so to speak, until they can resume fishing. Fishermen rarely take other jobs for the purpose of leaving the fishery.

COMMUNITY APPROACH

A fishing industry that includes a large number of part-time fishermen as envisioned under the community approach may be the most appropriate given the economic situation that exists in many coastal communities. Where occupational flexibility is a key component of the adaptive strategy, full-time fishermen will be unable or unlikely to maintain other employment options. When a downturn in the fishery reduces income and possibly forces a liquidation of quota shares, alternative employment may be difficult to find. Part-time fishermen, on the other hand, will be able to maintain multiple alternatives, either in other forms of employment or in access to other fisheries, a pattern not uncommon among fishermen even now.

Community-level managers will have better knowledge of the resources available to their members during down time in the fishery. For example, fishermen with more nonfishery options may be asked to forego a larger share of the quota with the promise of greater shares when the fishery recovers. These types of discretionary options would be impossible in a market approach. A fisherman forced to sell quota shares during downturns in the fishery may find it impossible to reenter the fishery during periods of increased stocks.

In summary, a market-based approach will reduce the flexibility of fishermen to engage in the traditional strategies of either switching fisheries or engaging in alternative employment during downturns in a particular fishery. In a market-based approach, fishermen unable to make a living during a brief downturn may be forced to leave the fishery permanently. Under community management, available resources can be allocated to allow the greatest number of fishermen the opportunity to remain viable during periodic downturns.

The Economic Pursuit of Quality

Fishing can be a critical component of a fisherman's income strategy, but it can also represent an important component of a community's economic structure. Development planners, especially those in small, non-urban communities that are typical of many coastal areas, are increasingly reorienting themselves away from single-source mega-employers that leave the entire area vulnerable to the vagaries of a rapidly changing and unpredictable world economy, and toward a more diversified, small-scale, multisource economy. Several analysts (e.g., Schumacher 1973; Power 1988; Daly and Cobb 1994) have been advocating just such an economic arrangement. Power, for example, argues that local development policies should be targeted to committed members of the community and that community development should focus on projects that improve the range and efficiency of the economic activities of local people.

Rather than measuring economic success in terms of GNP, communities' success should be measured by how well they satisfy people's real needs and wants: the availability of satisfying and useful work; security, as marked by access to biological and social necessities; stability; access to the qualities that make life varied, stimulating, and satisfying. Seen from this perspective, fishing is an ideal component of community economic development (Power 1988).

MARKET APPROACH

ITQs allocated through market mechanisms will not necessarily reflect the broader needs of the community—in fact, they probably will not do so. Quotas will flow to those with greatest access to the capital necessary to purchase them, an advantage that may have little correlation with community dependence on fishing. Small, rural coastal communities with the greatest reliance on fishing have less access to capital than do urban corporations. Access to the fishery will therefore be withdrawn from the very areas with the greatest reliance on fishing. The profits from the resources will likewise not return to the communities with the greatest reliance on marine resources, but will accrue to the corporate owners of quotas and their shareholders.

COMMUNITY APPROACH

Quotas allocated to and managed by communities would provide the communities with access, through their resident fishermen, to a valuable resource to augment their overall economic base. Communities with a vested interest in and need of marine resources would be guaranteed a share of the quota, thus contributing significantly to the maintenance and improvement of their own social and economic stability. Other sectors of the economy would benefit as well. The secondary and tertiary businesses directly linked to fishing would be guaranteed a customer base. Tourism, which in many coastal communities is linked to the fishing industry, would not be threatened with loss of a valuable asset. Overall, such stability would contribute greatly to the long-term social and economic health of communities that otherwise might not survive under a market-based approach. Under a community approach to management, fishing will continue to contribute to the factors outlined by Power that maintain and increase the economics of quality.

Implications of Different Forms
of Property Rights for Biological Management

The debates surrounding the relationships between property rights and natural resource use are still dynamic and evolving (Hanna, Folke, and Mäler 1996). Current market-based strategies tend to use a traditional land-based rationale for selecting property rights models. Sustainability in these models derives from the assumption that fishermen will have to protect the resource to their long-term benefit—a sort of "farming model" of resource management implying long-term stewardship.

MARKET APPROACH

Proponents of ITQs argue that conservation and sustainable resource use will result from the vested interest in sustainability that derives from ownership. Because quota holders no longer believe that "What I don't catch, somebody else will," they will be inclined to fish carefully and even forego fishing if holding off will yield market or other benefits. Since they have long-term predictable access to the fishery, they are more concerned with the long-term health of the stock. Fishermen will realize that sacrifices they make in the short term will be rewarded by long-term improvements in the value of their quota share (Buck 1995). The basic tenets of this type of model, however, may not be readily applicable to mobile, unpredictable, highly variable populations of fish. Like fishermen, farmers by no means face a predictable world. Farmers suffer the vagaries of weather and changing input and output prices. Like fishermen, farmers have incomes that vary from year to year due to factors well beyond their control. Unlike fishermen, however, farmers have exclusive access to a key basic resource—land. As such, they are secure in knowing that they, and no one else, will reap the benefits of any investments that are made. For example, application of fertilizer to improve soil productivity will benefit the farmer; if a particular area of land is left fallow, the farmer reaps the long-term benefits of this short-term sacrifice.

Such is not the case for fishermen. Holding a share of a quota only gives a particular fisherman a right or privilege to harvest fish. It confers no real control over the resource itself. The costs of any short-term sacrifices will be borne by the individual fishermen. The long-term benefits, however, will be shared by all participants in the fishery. Without coordinated effort, the incentives for improving the stock by any individual fisherman are dramatically reduced. By the same token, short-term benefits from actions such as high-grading, using damaging but productive fishing practices, or misreporting quota will accrue to the individual fisherman, while the long-term costs will be spread to all participants.

Long-term incentives may also be diluted by the unpredictability of the stock. Many factors besides fishing effort affect stock levels, a problem that has long hindered managers' attempts to predict the effects of their efforts. Long-term supply is unpredictable, and so there may be a considerable incentive to maximize returns on investment over the short term by maximizing resource extraction and then reinvesting the profits elsewhere. This problem will be most acute where the level of technology allows for highly destructive modes of fishing or where corporate owners are more attuned to fluctuating stock prices than to fluctuating stock levels. In this situation, short-term benefits accrue to one, while long-term costs are diffused to many. Taken together, these factors call into question the sustainability benefits of ITQs. The market may not be the best mechanism for assuring conservation and sustainability.

COMMUNITY APPROACHES

The characteristics of a community approach to management will mitigate the problems inherent in the market approach. A community approach is expected to include relatively large numbers of fishermen operating at a relatively small scale. Because these fishermen have an assured share of the quota through a community-based ITQ arrangement, they will be able to match technology to catch levels. The share is smaller, and so it is likely that these fishermen will also be utilizing smaller-scale technology. Levels of investment and dependency are lower in the community approach, and so incentives to destroy the ecosystem will be less. The destructive capacity of the technology will be reduced, and so the capacity to damage the environment will be less.

Face-to-face interaction will also enhance the opportunities for cooperation. If fishermen can be reasonably sure that they will share proportionally in the gains from short-term sacrifices such as habitat restoration or foregone catch, they are more likely to participate in such measures, particularly if they know and regularly interact with the other fishermen involved.

Another biological management advantage of the community approach is increased flexibility. Smaller-scale fishers with lower levels of investment in any individual fishery will have more flexibility to invest in multiple fisheries, a strategy commonly adopted in the face of uncertainty (Griffith and Dyer 1996). This practice will have the effect of reducing economic pressures on fishermen when low stock levels result in reduced quotas in a particular fishery, which in turn result in reduced pressure to set higher-than-biologically-optimal quota levels in the fishery. Managers at the community level will be in a better position to reallocate quotas from multiple fisheries in a fashion that best reflects local needs and conditions in the short term. Community-level managers will also be better able to even out short-term inequities in allocation than either higher-level managers or the market. A fisherman squeezed out by the market will have much less chance of reentering the fishery in a stock upturn than a fisherman who is a member of a community and who shares the cutbacks with others who allocate quotas so all can survive until better times.

Finally, economic development not related to fishing can have serious negative effects on the marine environment. Destructive pollution of coastal environments from construction and other activities can have serious implications for the health of the marine environment. As communities lose a vested interest in the marine environment through loss of fishing, they also lose an incentive to minimize damage to the marine environment. When communities derive direct economic benefit from the marine environment, they will be more interested in protecting its health. Management efforts that include the nonfishing elements of the community give more people an incentive to protect the marine environment, which will have important implications for the long-term health and sustainability of the resource.

SUMMARY

The management of fisheries, as with all natural resources, involves a complex interplay of a number of variables, some of which are biological but many of which are social and economic. ITQs have emerged as a promising solution to the problems of overcapitalization and overfishing that plague most of the world's fisheries. ITQs will eliminate several current problems, create new ones, exacerbate some, and have an indeterminate effect on others. The challenge is to sort out these impacts.

Economists have developed a model of human behavior that dramatically simplifies actual human behavior, and yet this simplified model has come to dominate decision making. The major proponents of ITQs have adopted it, leading them to envision quotas operating most effectively within the context of a free market adhering to the basic tenets of neoclassical economics. While such an approach *may* lead to the most efficient use of resources, it will do so at the cost of considerable worker displacement, community instability, and resource concentration.

Community approaches to fisheries management offer a realistic alternative to the market approach. Community management can build upon what is already an integral part of the fishing tradition. Fishing is a dangerous, uncertain occupation. While fishermen proclaim the virtues of individualism and competition, they realize full well that on the open seas, one's life may depend on one's competitor. Because they recognize their lack of control over the most basic aspects of their livelihood, fishermen place a high value on fair play. All suffer when some cheat. These two traits, mutual codependence and fair play, combine to create a strong sense of communal obligation that overrides the individualistic and competitive aspects of their profession during times of crisis, whether on the high seas or during economic hard times. Community approaches to management can build upon these traits, as well as the generalized traits of cooperation and mutual respect that exist in most groups of people, but economists have tended to disvalue these traits. Community-based approaches to managing ITQs offer opportunities to mitigate the social and potential environmental costs of ITQs while still reaping many of the most important benefits, particularly reduced fishing pressure and sustainable resource use.

Fishery management is a complex, uncertain business. Attempting to simplify it by applying inappropriate neoclassical economic models based on unrealistic assumptions will only lead to social disruption and the loss of irreplaceable human and social capital without achieving the sustainable use of valuable resources. In the headlong rush to privatize the resource, we may lose far more than we gain.

NOTES

1. See Dewar (1983) for an excellent and still timely review of this period in the New England Multispecies Groundfish Fishery, which is currently one of the most stressed fisheries from biological, economic, and social points of view.

2. The eight fishery management councils are the New England Council, with jurisdiction over the EEZ waters of Maine, New Hampshire, Massachusetts, Rhode Island, and Connecticut; the Mid-Atlantic Council, with jurisdiction in New York, New Jersey, Delaware, Pennsylvania, Maryland, Virginia, and North Carolina; the South Atlantic Council, with jurisdiction in North Carolina, South Carolina, Georgia, and Florida; the Gulf of Mexico Council, with jurisdiction in Texas, Louisiana, Mississippi, Alabama, and Florida; the Caribbean Council, with jurisdiction in the Virgin Islands and Puerto Rico; the Pacific Council, with jurisdiction in California, Washington, Oregon, and Idaho; the North Pacific Council, with jurisdiction in Alaska, Washington, and Or-

egon; and the Western Pacific Council, with jurisdiction in Hawaii, American Samoa, Guam, and the Northern Marianas Islands.

3. This description refers to how an ITQ system would operate under the simplest arrangements. Most ITQ systems have a number of restrictions over who may own shares, how shares can be transferred, what portion of the quota can be held by any individual/vessel, and so forth. For a review of many of these issues see Buck (1995). Three federal ITQ programs currently operate in the United States—for surf clam and ocean quahog in Mid-Atlantic and New England waters; for wreckfish along the South Atlantic coast; and for halibut and sablefish off Alaska. In 1986 New Zealand became the first nation to develop a major ITQ program. Other countries with ITQ management programs include Australia, Canada, Iceland, Italy, the Netherlands, and South Africa.

4. Part-time fishermen may include those who derive only a portion of their income from fishing and/or those who derive only a portion of their income from a *particular* fishery while working in one or more other fisheries.

REFERENCES

Betts, P. 1997. The Impact of the Fisheries Moratorium on Four Newfoundland Outport Communities. Paper presented at the annual meeting of the Society for Applied Anthropology, Seattle.

Binkley, M. 1997. The Changing Role of Women's Work in Nova Scotian Offshore Fishing Families. Paper presented at the annual meeting of the Society for Applied Anthropology, Seattle.

Brockway, G. 1995. *The End of Economic Man.* New York: Norton.

Buck, E. 1995. *Individual Transferable Quotas in Fishery Management: Congressional Research Service Report.* http://www.cnie.org/nle/mar-1.html.

Coastal Communities Network of Nova Scotia (CCN). 1997. *Co-management.* http://www.gdlewis.ednet.ns.ca/~coastal/coman.html.

Conover, K. 1998. East Coast Chefs No Longer Hooked on Serving Swordfish. *Christian Science Monitor,* January 29: B-1.

Crowley, B. L. 1996. *Taking Ownership: How to Make the Atlantic Fishery an Engine of Economic Growth.* New York: Atlantic Institute for Market Studies.

Daly, H. E., and J. B. Cobb. 1994. *For the Common Good: Redirecting the Economy toward Community, the Environment, and a Sustainable Future.* 2d ed. Boston: Beacon Press.

Dewar, M. 1983. *Industry in Trouble.* Philadelphia: Temple University Press.

Economic Policy Institute (EPI). 1997. *Nonstandard Work, Substandard Jobs: Flexible Work Arrangements in the United States.* Washington, D.C.: Economic Policy Institute.

Edwards, S., and S. Murawski. 1993. Potential Economic Benefits from Efficient Harvest of New England Groundfish. *North American Journal of Fishery Management* 13:437–49.

Food and Agriculture Organization (FAO). 1993. *Marine Fisheries and the Law of the Sea: A Decade of Change.* Rome: Food and Agriculture Organization.

Griffith, D., and C. L. Dyer. 1996. *An Appraisal of the Social and Cultural Aspects of the Multispecies Groundfish Fishery in New England and the Mid-Atlantic Regions.* Silver Spring, Md.: National Oceanographic and Atmospheric Administration.

Hallowell, C. 1998. Save the Swordfish. *Time,* January 26: 48.

Hanna, S. S., C. Folke, and K-G Mäler. 1996. *Rights to Nature: Ecological, Economic, Cultural, and Political Principles of Institutions for the Environment.* Washington, D.C.: Island Press.

Harré, R., D. Clark, and N. de Carlo. 1985. *Motives and Mechanisms.* London: Methuen.

Koch, J. V. 1976. *Microeconomic Theory and Applications.* Boston: Little, Brown.

McCay, B. J. 1987. The Culture of the Commoners: Historical Observations on Old and New World Fisheries. In *The Question of the Commons,* ed. B. J. McCay and J. M. Acheson, pp. 195–216. Tucson: University of Arizona Press.

McGoodwin, J. R. 1991. *Crisis in the World's Fisheries: People, Problems, and Policies.* Stanford, Calif.: Stanford University Press.

McQuaid, J. 1996. Overfished Waters Running on Empty. In *Oceans of Trouble,* ed. J. McQuaid, B. Marshall, M. Schleifstein, and T. Jackson, pp. 15–25. New Orleans: Times–Picayune Press.

Pauley, D., J. Dalsgaard, V. Christensen, R. Froese, and F. Torres. 1998. Fishing Down Marine Food Webs. *Science,* February 6: 60–65.

Power, T. M. 1988. *The Economic Pursuit of Quality.* Armonk, N.Y.: Sharp Press.

Schumacher, E. F. 1973. *Small Is Beautiful: Economics as If People Mattered.* New York: Harper and Row.

Thurow, L. 1984. *Dangerous Currents.* New York: Random House.

United Nations Development Programme (UNDP). 1994. *Human Development Report.* New York: Oxford University Press.

U.S. Department of Commerce (USDOC). 1995. *Our Living Oceans.* Washington, D.C.: U.S. Department of Commerce, National Oceanographic and Atmospheric Administration, and National Marine Fisheries Service.

———1996. *Our Living Oceans.* Washington, D.C.: U.S. Department of Commerce, National Oceanographic and Atmospheric Administration, and National Marine Fisheries Service.

Weber, P. 1994. *Net Loss: Fish, Jobs, and the Marine Environment.* Washington, D.C.: Worldwatch Institute.

Down on the Clam Farm: Aquaculture, Privatization, and Sacred Space in the Core Banks Shellfish Lease Controversy, North Carolina

Barbara J. Garrity-Blake

Studies of the growth and globalization of aquaculture have revealed links between this mode of food production and environmental degradation, increased poverty, and social dislocation, particularly in developing countries that host expanding maritime farm operations (Stonich, Bort, and Ovares 1997; Pollnac and Weeks 1992; Meltzoff and LiPuma 1986). Competition from farmed imports has resulted in a lowering of market prices, a hardship for U.S. fishers (Maril 1995; Durrenberger 1994).

Few studies, however, have examined how the expansion of aquacultural enterprises within the United States has transformed coastal communities and led to the proliferation of industries related to leisure and marine science.[1] Domestically grown seafood is often touted as the answer to declining wild commercial harvests, but the growth of aquaculture can itself lead to declines in seafood harvests due to such political and economic factors as the allocation of work space away from commercial fishers in favor of those seeking to lease public resource waters for shellfish beds.

Recent proposals to lease acreage in the pristine waters off an uninhabited North Carolina barrier island called Core Banks triggered a heated public protest. The controversy exposed fracture lines between those who harvest wild fish and shellfish (commercial fishermen) and those who participate in aquacultured or farm-grown shellfish production (shellfish farmers). Contested ideas of what constitutes productivity and public benefit are central to the Core Banks clam lease issue.

Commercial fishers demonstrate a strong aversion to the privatization of public resource waters in general, but their reaction to the Core Banks lease proposals reflects a specific concern with that island and its surrounding waters, which constitute a sacred landscape to local Down East families. The potential privatization of Core Banks for shellfish leasing contradicts cultural ideas about identity, freedom, and sanctity.

DOWN EAST

The western half of Carteret County, North Carolina, with the ever-developing "Crystal Coast" resort and retirement havens of Emerald Isle, Pine Knoll Shores, and Beaufort, is prosperous. By contrast, the far eastern or "Down East" portion of the county consists of low marshland with a long string of unincorporated villages. The local commercial fishing families are known for their distinctive "Elizabethan" dialect (Wolfram and Schilling-Estes 1997), their devotion to church and family, and their tenacious spirit of independence, exemplified by the occasional call for Down East to secede from the rest of the county.[2]

Down East fishing families employ a variety of techniques to harvest several kinds of fish and seafood, many of which are caught in the "inside" waters of Core and Pamlico Sounds, as opposed to the "outside" waters of the Atlantic Ocean. Fishermen who run small-scale independent operations in search of shrimp, jumping mullet, croaker, spot, scallops, oysters, and clams are known locally as the "little fellers," distinct from the "big fellers" who work on company-owned, ocean-going vessels (Garrity-Blake 1994). Fishermen who clam do so with hand rakes or mechanical methods such as dredging or "clam kicking." Many became involved in the state's shellfish relay program, securing small leases to transport clams from polluted areas so that the shellfish could purge themselves and become marketable.

Growing clams and oysters in leased public trust waters is not a new endeavor in coastal North Carolina. In fact, the state had 2,170 acres of estuary, sound, and bay bottom leased to some 300 people in 1998, although a rising trend is indicated by the level of capital investment in aquaculture, the amount of grant money allocated to shellfish farmers and scientists, and proposed legislative changes designed to promote private shellfish production in public trust waters. In fact, a blue ribbon committee was appointed by the governor to address the problem of shellfish diseases; it recommended expanding private maritime farming operations and revising leasing procedures to make it easier for aquacultural enterprises to get started. It also recommended $700,000 toward new research facilities and $1.3 million toward state-funded aquaculture studies (NCBRACO 1995). Fishermen, however, were concerned that the committee missed the point: how, they wanted to know, could pollution and declining water quality (both of which problems have resulted in the closure of shellfish beds) be offset?

Relatively new to the Down East area are those who have invested capital to develop and maintain shellfish farms on a full-time basis. The largest of these enterprises involve experimental seed hatchery facilities with raceways and nursery systems, as well as bottom leases in public trust waters to plant and cultivate clams and/or oysters. Some of these operations have obtained hard-to-come-by water column leases from the state; not only is the bottom acreage itself off-limits to the public, but so is the water column over the lease site.

In Atlantic and Sea Level, two adjoining Down East fishing villages, the word "aquaculture" has become synonymous with the name of Sam Nelson,[3] who launched one of the most successful clam hatcheries in the state. Once he secured a lease along the shore near his Atlantic home, Nelson became involved in state-funded research projects, working in conjunction with the University of North Carolina Institute for Marine Science. Despite local rumors that he was living off taxpayers' money, Nelson built an impressive three-story house in the middle of a community whose residents still abide by a cultural etiquette that frowns on any display of prosperity not shared by one's neighbors.

Much to the chagrin of local fishermen, Nelson has served on various shellfish and fisheries management committees for the state. He is known to present himself to legislators as a born-again fisherman who has forsaken the traditional "destructive" techniques of wild harvesting in favor of the clean, scientific approach of aquaculture, the "wave of the future" (Rich 1996). The last straw for Down East fishing families, however, was when Nelson proposed to expand his operations in 1992 to include ten acres of public trust bottom just off Core Banks. They argued that Nelson wanted what many consider to be "too much for one man," and they expressed the fear that his unprecedented request would open the door for other aquaculturalists to lay claim to an area that many believe should remain public and inalienable.

Core Banks, the thin strip of sand across the sound, is visible from most Down East communities. It was designated a national park in 1966;

with Portsmouth Island and Shackleford Banks, Core Banks now makes up the Cape Lookout National Seashore. Before it fell under the jurisdiction of the federal government, however, people owned land and cabins on Core Banks, some of which are still held until lifetime leases run out. Many families are direct descendants of the Core Bankers, who lived in permanent fishing and whaling villages until fierce storms in the 1890s led them to relocate to the mainland. Down East families continue to make frequent pilgrimages to Core Banks for weekend excursions, during which they teach their children how to swim and sign (find) clams in the safety of the shallow sound waters.

The opposition to the leasing of Core Banks waters included a petition with more than 800 names; nevertheless, the state granted Nelson 7.1 acres of Core Banks bottom, although it also declared a two-year moratorium on new lease applications in Core Sound while the situation was studied.[4] By the time the moratorium was set to expire, several applications were submitted for adjoining ten-acre leases off Core Banks, including ten more for Nelson and ten for his daughter. In all, by 1996 over seventy acres of Core Banks bottom, desirable to shellfish farmers for its shallow, clean waters, was proposed for leasing.

This decision resulted in a flood of letters to local newspapers and state officials, legal action on behalf of those on both sides of the issue, and emotional testimony at a jam-packed public hearing at which more than 400 sworn protests were submitted. Although the North Carolina Division of Marine Fisheries only recognized 65 of the 400 protests as having a legitimate right to address specific criteria, legislators were impressed by the numbers. Before the Division acted on the leases, the North Carolina General Assembly passed new legislation declaring that no new leases could be granted along Core Banks, with the exception of Nelson's original 7.1-acre lease.

PRODUCTIVITY AND THE PUBLIC GOOD

To approve a lease application, the Division of Marine Fisheries must show that the proposed site does not support commercially viable populations of naturally occurring shellfish. The state defines productive bottom as yielding ten or more bushels of shellfish per acre. Sampling of Sam Nelson's original proposed lease yielded only 1.4 bushels of clams per acre, well under what would be required to deny him the lease.

Fishermen questioned the state's definition of productive bottom, pointing out that what the state considers barren can still provide a "decent day's work" to someone with a bucket and a clam rake. But "one bushel of clams will equal 250 chowder clams, 400 cherrystone clams, or 600 littleneck clams," wrote a woman. "At ten cents each, 1.4 bushels [sampled on Nelson's lease] would earn a clammer [an average of] $56. I think . . . many clammers would consider $56 a decent day's work." William W. Cobey Jr., then secretary of the Department of Environment, Health, and Natural Resources, responded, "A natural shellfish bed is ten bushels an acre, not a decent day's work as you describe" (NCDMF 1992).

Fishermen also questioned the state's sampling methods, charging that the Division of Marine Fisheries based its investigation on one day of sampling per lease, which does not reflect how clam abundance varies from month to month, week to week, or even day to day. Fishermen also pointed out that the Core Banks samples were taken in cool months, too early in the season to reflect true abundance, and included large expanses of sandy bottom, rather than grassy areas where clams are known to congregate. "There are a lot of places that are sandy bottom and the clams are not catcheable . . . due to cold water, northerly winds, and so on," wrote a fisherman. "My father and myself have tried many a place in winter and late spring and caught nothing only to go back a month or two later and do good clamming. The Banks is a funny place, catch some one day, the next nothing" (NCDMF 1992). Overall, fishermen claimed that state employees simply did not know how to find clams, and so productive shellfish bottom is continually leased out to private interests.

Acknowledging fishermen's doubts as to the state's ability to find clams, the Division of Marine Fisheries agreed to a supplementary investigation of the Core Banks sites with the participation of local fishermen. The supplemental report stated that the fishermen were unfamiliar with the use of the sampling frames and that they shared a firmly held belief that clams could not be raked from bare, sandy bottom at certain times of the year. The fishermen dug in sea grass areas, finding a much higher density of clams than state workers had uncovered, but still under the ten bushels required to deny a lease. The report conceded, however, that this result does point out the need for a further assessment of the suitability of leasing the sea grass areas contained in the proposed lease sites (NCDMF 1996b).

Another major point of contention involved the definition of "public benefit." A state statute declares that a lease may be granted when it is determined that "the public interest will benefit" from its issuance. The primary public benefit, according to growers and scientists, is that filter-feeding shellfish help clean impurities out of the water; they also produce spawn, which drifts into public areas and thus restocks those areas with new clams or oysters.[5]

Fishers took issue with these claims, particularly the assertion that farm-grown shellfish help restock wild beds. They pointed out that wild clams do so as well as, if not better than, farmed clams because the minimum size for wild clams is one inch, ensuring that clams reach maturity for spawning, whereas farmed clams may be harvested at any size, including the profitable and tender small ones. "I feel a lease would not help us as one of those biologists said it would," wrote a fisherman. "He said that the clams on the lease would spawn and drift to other areas. . . . [Well,] the clam that spawns is the [large] cherry[stone], worth [only] six or seven cents on a good market, whereas the [smaller] little-neck brings ten to fourteen cents. People who have leases harvest the [more valuable littleneck] clams . . . which is . . . not a spawner" (NCDMF 1992). Fishermen also questioned the ability of farmed clams to clean impurities out of the water. Some pointed out that farmed clams are planted in densities thicker than those typical of the natural beds, and so they are likely to produce waste in higher concentrations.

Overall, Down East residents questioned the logic that construes the privatization of fisheries' resources as public benefit. "Clammers and all fishermen need places to work," wrote a man. "You are taking the bottom away from hundreds of commercial fishermen that have the right to clam and set nets across this body of water," said another. "If this is allowed to continue, a handful of people will control the water and everyone else will have to search elsewhere" (NCDMF 1992).

CORE BANKS AS SACRED LANDSCAPE

The opposition to clam leases on Core Banks stems from an antipathy toward privatization and from differing ideas as to what constitutes "productivity." There is also the matter of small-community dislike of one of the personalities involved in expanding aquaculture. But most of the letters, sworn statements, and public testimony made it clear that protests were not directed at Sam Nelson or the activity of aquaculture per se; rather, it was the *site* of the proposed leases that was most unacceptable.

It is evident that Core Banks is more than a work area for Down East residents; it is a landscape charged with symbolism for local families. Indeed, according to the North Carolina Division of Marine Fisheries, the "general theme apparent in the majority of the [Core Banks] protests was a concern over the loss of, or endangerment to, the heritage and traditions of the Down East communities that have utilized the Outer Banks for generations" (NCDMF 1996a). "Core Banks is sacred to us. . . . These Outer Banks and shores and shoals are like a retreat to many a troubled mind and a peace to the soul," testified a woman at the lease hearing. "You'll never be any closer to God than when you see the wonders of God's home and his love for mankind than on the Banks' shoals" (NCDMF 1996c).

"My great-grandfather, Charles A. Mason, and his wife, Louisa, owned forty-two acres . . . on Core Banks," declared a woman at the lease hearings. "[He turned it over] to the U.S. government . . . [for] a life-saving [station] . . . [and it is] now the National Seashore. It was his intention that it never be owned by no one individual, but it be there for everybody" (NCDMF 1996c). The federal acquisition of the banks created hard feelings among families who had to relinquish their land and cabins, but the spirit of public trust is accepted in regard to the land and, until recently, taken for granted in regard to the waters.

"You have all the Park Service rules you have to go by just to spend time on the Outer Banks," wrote a fisherman's wife, expressing a concern for the appropriation of space and loss of freedom. "Now to let someone have so-called private waters on the Outer Banks would be putting the icing on the cake. . . . It is bad enough you have to know where you can get your feet wet on the mainland side without getting shot, now you will have to beware of where you walk on the banks" (NCDMF 1996c).

Core Banks is also thought to represent God's good will toward the "down and out," a sort of sanctified safety net against hunger and poverty. For a community distrustful of government and notoriously disinclined to seek social services, the "hand of God" provides, for one can always find food or income "pushing a clam rake" when all else fails. "I've seen all these men and women in here making livings, raise their babies," said a woman. "I think the Lord made that water for everybody.

. . . I think about up in New York City people starve to death. . . . When we get hungry here, if we can't make a living, we can go out there with a clam rake and we can catch something to eat" (NCDMF 1996c). "A person that wants to work can invest in a skiff, a clam rake, a washtub, an inner tube and be in the clam fishery without a lot of money being spent," wrote a Down East man. "Men and women are out there pushing a clam rake because they do not have the education to do anything else," advised another (NCDMF 1996c).

For those living on the eastern edge of Carteret County, a look west reveals heavy urban development, bureaucracy, politics, and regulations. A look east reveals calm waters protected by the sandy arms of the Outer Banks, the last frontier of freedom for those who feel their backs are against the wall in a rapidly changing coastal economy. "If you people would look around and see how much territory has already been taken away from the fisherman!" testified a man. "[They took all] the land along the waterfront. You can't work around a pier. You can't go up rivers or nothing 'cause them people they took that land. Why in the world do you want to take [Core Banks] away from the public and give it to just two or three people?" (NCDMF 1996c). For these coastal southerners who so strongly identify with both the local geography and their occupation, the "wave of the future" on Core Banks promises cultural erosion and economic loss.

The privatization of public trust waters via leasing is often promoted as the solution to alleged unbridled exploitation of common property resources (McCay and Acheson 1987). Nevertheless, the growth of domestic shellfish farming presents a concern to small-scale commercial fishing households because it results in the loss of harvesting areas. The matter is more complex, however, than competition for resources. The controversy surrounding the Core Banks shellfish lease proposals illustrates the interwoven nature of culture, landscape, and economy. Core Banks and its surrounding waters is not only an environmental or economic resource to be fought over but a symbolic landscape charged with meanings pertaining to a people's sense of identity and place in a rapidly changing coastal community.

NOTES

1. The linkages between leisure development, marine science, aquaculture, and the decline of fishing deserve further study.

2. One call to secede occurred in the early 1990s when the densely developed resort town of Atlantic Beach proposed piping its wastewater to Open Grounds Farm, which includes most of the acreage of Down East. Down East residents saw this move as a literal as well as a symbolic case of the rich dumping on the poor.

3. A pseudonym.

4. The North Carolina Division of Marine Fisheries modified Nelson's request of 10 acres to 7.1 acres because of charges that "significant concentrations of hard clams existed just outside the proposed lease boundaries" (NCDMF 1992).

5. Another touted benefit was designed to appeal to the powerful sport fishing lobby: the dumped oyster shells would create reefs and improve fishing.

REFERENCES

Durrenberger, E. P. 1994. *It's All Politics: South Alabama's Seafood Industry.* Urbana: University of Illinois Press.

Garrity-Blake, B. J. 1994. *The Fish Factory: Work and Meaning for Black and White Fishermen of the American Menhaden Industry.* Knoxville: University of Tennessee Press.

McCay, B. J., and J. M. Acheson. 1987. Human Ecology of the Commons. In *The Question of the Commons,* ed. B. J. McCay and J. M. Acheson, pp. 1–36. Tucson: University of Arizona Press.

Maril, R. L. 1995. *The Bay Shrimpers of Texas: Rural Fishermen in a Global Economy.* Lawrence: University of Kansas Press.

Meltzoff, S. K., and E. LiPuma. 1986. The Social and Political Economy of Coastal Zone Management: Shrimp Mariculture in Ecuador. *Coastal Zone Management Journal* 14:349–80.

North Carolina Blue Ribbon Advisory Council on Oysters (NCBRACO). 1995. *Final Report: Findings and Recommendations.* Raleigh: NCBRACO.

North Carolina Division of Marine Fisheries (NCDMF). 1992. *Letters re: Core Banks Lease #9201.* Raleigh: NCDMF.

———. 1996a. *Memorandum to the Director, April 8.* Raleigh: NCDMF.

———. 1996b. *Memorandum to the Director, April 11.* Raleigh: NCDMF.

———. 1996c. *Transcript of Public Hearing on Proposed Core Banks Shellfish Leases, April 8.* Raleigh: NCDMF.

Pollnac, R., and P. Weeks, eds. 1992. *Coastal Aquaculture in Developing Countries: Problems and Prospects.* Kingston, R.I.: International Commission on Marine Resources Development.

Rich, B. 1996. Water War: It's Science versus Tradition in Battle over State Clam Leases. *Carteret News-Times,* April 7:A-2.

Stonich, S. C., J. R. Bort, and L. L. Ovares. 1997. Globalization of Shrimp Mariculture: The Impact on Social Justice and Environmental Quality in Central America. *Society and Natural Resources* 10:161–79.

Wolfram, W., and N. Schilling-Estes. 1997. *Hoi Toide on the Outer Banks.* Chapel Hill: University of North Carolina Press.

Licenses and Livelihoods: Changing Fishing Economy in a Malay Village

Margaret W. Kedia

This article describes the impact of the expanding global economy on a fishing community in Malaysia.[1] The pressures of the market economy and the declining income from fishing have profoundly affected the local fishermen, many of whom are encouraging their children to opt for other occupations. Due to globalization of the local economy, there are new perceptions and expectations of material culture coupled with an increasing need for cash to meet the demands of daily life. With the availability of factory jobs and employment with corporations backed by international capital, the occupation of fishing has been relegated to an inferior status. Compared with fishing, working for the corporations or their affiliates is considered more prestigious, which is equated with "modern" and "developed." The combination of financial pressures, declining income from fishing, and public perceptions regarding fishing has resulted in an antipathy toward fishing among many of the younger generation. They tend to pursue any income-generating activity other than fishing. Despite the fact that these fishing communities are ideally situated to make use of the local marine resources, the current trend of global economic expansion may lead to the gradual demise of the traditional fishing economy.

RESEARCH SETTING

This study was carried out in a fishing community that includes three villages located very close together in the district of Kemaman, in the state of Terengganu, which borders the South China Sea along the east coast of Malaysia. There are more than 1,100 households in the three interlinked villages, two of which are government-sponsored resettlements for people who have lost their homes to the waves or who are landless. The first resettlement was begun in the 1950s and the second in the 1990s. In spite of the resettlements, the population in both villages seems to have increased with migrants from more northerly parts of the state. Fishermen have been attracted to the area because of the ease of docking along the river that borders two of the villages; even when waves are high at sea (a frequent occurrence during the monsoon season), the river mouth remains calm.

The inhabitants are ethnic Malays. They are Muslims, and many are being influenced by Islamic revivalism. Malays practice bilateral kinship, and households tend to consist of nuclear families, although they frequently include additional relatives (e.g., grandparents, grandchildren, nieces, and nephews). For purposes of this analysis, a household is defined as a group of individuals, usually kin, who form a cooperative economic unit that shares activities and resources in some way (Netting, Wilk, and Arnould 1984; Smith 1984). In this community, many young men and women desire to live independently after marriage but lack the resources to do so. Many newly married couples start by living in the house of one set of parents or in their own house on their parents' property. The child who is going to take care of the parents in their old age often continues to live with them even after marriage.

One of the most striking aspects of family life in this community is the large number of children. The average couple has about ten children, which is well above the current norm in Malaysia. It is not unusual for couples to have a few grandchildren born around the same time as their own younger children. Women in their early thirties may already have six children. Although both men and women are now marrying at a later age, they still want at least six or seven children. The large number of children is associated with increasing financial stress on the households.

The local economy is being transformed by global economic forces. Until the recent financial crisis in Asia, Malaysia for decades had an impressive record of attracting international capital, particularly through the establishment of foreign-owned export-oriented industries (Tsuruoka 1992; Balakrishnan 1989; Jomo 1993). National policymakers promoted the foreign-owned industries as a symbol of modernization and as the engine of growth that would transform Malaysia into the next Newly Industrialized Country (NIC) by the year 2020, according to the prime minister (Mahathir 1991). In the research community, economic globalization is most visible in the expansion of industries that hire both men and women. These industries are a mix of multinational and national, but the latter also tend to be backed by international capital. The factories that hire women are primarily producers of electronics, furniture, and plywood. Men are employed by industrial plants, including those producing steel and its by-products, at an industrial port, and by furniture and ice-making plants. Many men work on contracts to provide services associated with these plants, such as driving lorries or operating canteens. The establishment of industry has stimulated the growth of the service sector. Material culture has grown rapidly as people become increasingly tied to the market economy. The nearby town is bustling and congested with traffic.

The research community is separated from the town only by a river, although it gives the initial appearance of being sheltered from the penetration of the global economy. Most striking is its relative lack of affluence. One frequently hears how the community is "bypassed by development." But in reality, the market economy is gradually encroaching on the lives of the villagers. Young people are finding jobs with the newly established industries. More people than ever before have motorized vehicles, especially motorcycles but also some cars, and lorries and passenger vans constantly use the main road through the community. More people than ever have disposable cash. Some women who are not working in the factories are starting their own small businesses. Parents are insisting that children stay in school longer so that they will have a chance to succeed in the changing economic environment.

The research was conducted for ten months in 1995–96, when I lived in the community.[2] Fishing is central to the community's identity and pace of life. Since I am a woman and only men fish (and much of the infrastructure and activities surrounding fishing are "male space"), most of the information presented here was collected through observation, informal discussions, and a few in-depth interviews. In addition, a socioeconomic survey was conducted for sixty households either by myself or by a field assistant.

THE FISHING ECONOMY

Fishermen have traditionally worked on boats owned by the Chinese middlemen who bought their fish. The fishermen had to sell their fish at noncompetitive prices because they were in debt to these middlemen (Firth 1966; Aziz 1959). Circumstances changed in the 1970s with a government program that assisted fishermen in buying their own boats and nets.[3] The fishermen consequently gained ownership, and the level of their technology was upgraded. Almost all their boats now have in-board motors. In 1987 the Department of Fisheries built a fishing complex that includes a concrete jetty with overhead roof, petrol pumps, and ice-grinding machines; it also houses local offices for the Department of Fisheries and its sponsored fishermen's union, a row of offices for fish dealers, a parking lot, and a tiled marketplace for local retail fish sales. Although fishermen's livelihoods have improved considerably, they are still perceived as "backwards" and poor.

Approximately 600 fishermen in the community are registered with the local branch of the Department of Fisheries. The community has a strong fishermen's cooperative, started in 1957; roughly half of the community's fishermen are members. The cooperative is a major social and economic influence in the community and a place for fishermen to share information and to pool their resources for technologically advanced equipment, which can result in increased profit. The most notable function of the cooperative is to act as a middleman, buying fish from the fishermen and selling the catch to merchants at markets elsewhere. There is also a fishermen's union that sells petrol and ice to the fishermen at a discounted rate. Many fishermen are members of both organizations, but the cooperative is by far the more active body.

The fishing economy is structured around the annual monsoon season, which starts in late October and lasts until early February. For those with the smallest boats, it is a period of shortfall, when household resources must be stretched to last until the fishermen can once again go to sea. For those who have larger boats and gear suitable to working on the high seas, it is a time of plenty because the most profitable catch, prawns, are in season. Either way, the monsoon is significant for fishermen's household economies.

Technology

The fact that fishermen in this community tend to use relatively small boats is often cited as an example of their "backwardness." Small boats must return daily, while larger ones can be at sea for several days at a time. The typical boat holds a crew of four to six, and it can travel about ten miles from shore. All boats from this area have the same general appearance, with a shape distinctive to the region.

There is, however, considerable variation in the types of gear people use to catch fish. There are various kinds of nets, hooks, lines, and traps. Only trawl and purse-seine nets are considered commercial gear, while all others have been part of the traditional apparatus. The fishermen modify their nets after purchase from the factory; nets are cut, sections added or deleted, and buoys or weights are attached so that the net operates to suit the particular fisherman. Many fishermen use more than one type of gear, depending on the season. They are most likely to trade in their usual net for one appropriate for catching shrimp during the winter months when the monsoon winds and waves stir the shellfish off the sea bottom, making them easier to catch.

Natural Resource Management

Malaysia's Department of Fisheries is responsible for managing the marine resources in the surrounding seas by means of licensing, enforcement, and development of marine resources. The ultimate goal is to develop aquaculture. Licenses are issued separately for boats and gear and are renewed annually. Boats are licensed according to size. Most fishermen in the community have licenses for the smallest size, known as Category A. Someone with a license A is permitted to go anywhere, but in practice he cannot travel far from shore. A boat with the next size license, Category B, may not fish within five miles of the shore. Boats with licenses C and C2 may not fish less than twelve and thirty miles from shore, respectively. There is a marine police force to make sure that boats fish in accordance with what their licenses permit. In the community, only a small number have license B; there are no C licenses, and only one C2.

The Department of Fisheries also issues licenses for gear. Persons with boats licensed B or larger can obtain a license for only one type of gear, almost always a trawl or purse-seine net. Fishermen with license A boats can have multiple licenses for different types of gear, usually involving a mixture of nets that vary by hole size, thread thickness, and the number of buoys and weights attached. The gear is designed to catch specific fish according to the season.

It is difficult to assess the effectiveness of the licensing. The Marine Fishery Resources Development and Management Division of the Southeast Asian Fisheries Development Center has found signs of overfishing in Zone B waters, but not in Zone C or C2.[4] No research has been done for Zone A because the Center assumes that traditional gear cannot deplete fish resources. Because of these findings, the Department of Fisheries restricts B licenses, but not those for other zones.

Many local fishermen view the licensing policies as insufficient because the fish supply is actually decreasing, even in Zone A. There is no consensus as to the cause of this decrease, but some fishermen see the marine resources in the licensed zones as interconnected and blame the larger boats for taking all the fish, including babies and eggs. Most people credit at least some of the depletion in the fish supply to policies and practices beyond the control of the Department of Fisheries, including the government's dredging of sand from the nearby sea bed to build an industrial port. There have also been problems with oil spills and chemical discharge from some of the factories along the shore. These problems are all linked with attempts to encourage globalization of the economy, which often works to the detriment of effective marine resource management.

The licensing policy is also seen as restrictive because those with a license A cannot upgrade to license B. It can be quite expensive to purchase the larger boat that would justify a license upgrade, and so it is unlikely that a fisherman could ever accumulate enough to upgrade two levels, from A to C, even though those with licenses B or C regularly upgrade.

It is misleading, however, to think that the fishermen want to operate the largest possible boats. The Fishermen's Cooperative itself owns two large fishing vessels, but it hires Thais to work on them because local fishermen are unwilling to do so. People explain the local fishermen's reluctance to work on the large boats by saying that "they are not developed enough," meaning that they are parochial and not forward-looking. This characterization reinforces the notion that the fishermen are "backwards," as demonstrated through their use of small-scale technology. This view, however, overlooks the fact that there are aspects of the very large boats that are considered undesirable. Most men in the community prefer to work for themselves, and they will opt for working on a contract basis with a local sawmill, even at the risk of uncertainty of pay and lack of benefits, rather than work for a fixed wage. Working for someone else is referred to as *ikat,* which means "tied." A man who works on a large boat would be working for someone else rather than being his own boss; he would not be an equal working in cooperation with other fishermen. Moreover, the large boats are away from shore for several days at a time, sometimes up to ten days or two weeks. Working on the large boats thus disrupts family and community activities. The Malay fishermen also object to working with Thais, because the latter cook pork, which the Muslim Malays are forbidden to eat; they do not even like to be in an environment in which it is being prepared for others to eat. Some fishermen do want to upgrade their licenses, but do not really want to have a boat that would be too large to allow them to return daily. The problem is that the boats that would be larger but still small enough to allow for daily return are the ones that would collect fish in the areas already most depleted.

The perception of the impact of the restriction in license upgrades is not uniform. Both fishermen in the community and the Department of Fisheries say that the size of the boat has nothing to do with a fisherman's success. A fisherman with a size A boat may find as much as one with a size B boat; he may sometimes even do better. The real determining factor is the fisherman's skill. There are others in the community, including some whose applications for a larger boat license have been denied, who point out the irony of their being branded "backwards" because they use such small boats, even though they are denied "development" by a government that restricts their access to larger boats.

Marketing

About half of the fish landed are sold to the Fishermen's Cooperative, which in turn sells them to merchants in Kuala Lumpur and Singapore. It is not necessary to be a member in order to sell to the Cooperative, and the latter does not prevent its members from selling elsewhere if they wish. Several private dealers buy fish directly from the fishermen and sell them at the major markets in Singapore, Kuala Lumpur, and Johore Baharu (a Malaysian city across the river from Singapore). In addition, there are a few men who purchase small quantities of fish to sell at the afternoon market located next to the jetty. People from nearby towns, rather than members of the community, shop at this market.

Globalization is reflected in the marketing of fish. Just about half of the fish caught (with some slight seasonal variations) are exported to Singapore. Most fish species are sold either to Singapore or to Kuala Lumpur, but there are some species that are sold to both. The costlier fish are typically sold in Singapore.

Despite the negative perception of small boats, the small-scale technology allows fishermen in the community to find a niche for their product. Fish caught by these small boats are generally fresh (arriving at the market within twenty-four hours of being caught) and of high quality, and they can command substantially higher market prices than fish gathered by the large boats, which are often dragged in nets for long distances and then stored for several days before they reach land. Indeed, the lowest price of the fish from this community is well above the average market price for the rest of Malaysia. The market demand for fresh fish and the willingness to pay for that quality are often overlooked factors that belie the "backwards" stereotype of the community's fishing enterprise. Nevertheless, the income that can be derived from the large boats is, in the long run, larger than that from the small boats. The one person in the community who owns a large boat can make anywhere between RM$900 and RM$2,000 a month after paying his crew, in contrast to a monthly range of RM$400–600 for those using smaller boats.[5]

TRENDS ACCOMPANYING GLOBALIZATION

There are two important trends associated with the globalization of the local economy: an increased need for individuals and household heads to have disposable cash, and a changing perception of what constitutes a desirable job, with factory employment being positively evaluated and fishing being negatively assessed.

Globalization, particularly the establishment of factories in the area, has brought about inflation. The cost of basic goods (e.g., rice, sugar, tea) increased noticeably during the period of research. There is also what might be called "social inflation," which refers to the increased expectations people have for what a basic lifestyle should include, with many more goods, once viewed as luxuries, now considered necessities. Without these goods, someone is considered poor and deprived. A well-off family used to be one that had enough to eat during the monsoon season. Now, if a family meets that standard, it is considered poor.

There are economic expenditures associated with social and infrastructural changes, including changes in housing, amenities, marriage, and education. Before the 1970s, there was no piped water, electricity, or phone service. These amenities are nice to have and increase the standard of living, but they are also costly. With the exception of the telephone, the monthly expenditures for these amenities are small, but the cost is cumulative. Land is highly regulated; titles and territory are set aside for government ownership. Whereas a generation ago people settled on unoccupied land that they cleared for themselves, they are no longer permitted to occupy any clear piece of land they find. In addition to neolocal residence being the cultural norm, families have many children—too many for most to live in their parents' house after marriage. Most younger people must rent a place to live, a substantial added monthly expense. Land ownership, by contrast, did not incur regular expenditure, as there were no property taxes in the state.

Globalization of the local economy is accompanied by social changes that carry economic costs. For example, even if there is no elaborate wedding ceremony, the amount of bridewealth paid to the bride's family has increased dramatically in the last decade at a rate that far outstrips increases in income. In addition, the traditional gift exchanges (*gubahan*) between the bride and groom at both the engagement and marriage ceremonies have become more elaborate in content and in number of items. Many items exchanged are prescribed by custom and frequently require time to prepare, although with the exception of gold rings and the bridewealth itself, they need not be very expensive. But items beyond the traditional set can reflect a new consumerism. Goods only recently available in the expanding market economy that may now be added to the exchange include toiletries wrapped in wax paper, shoes, handbags, and material for a dressy outfit. These goods can be quite expensive, with the minimum cost for an individual item being close to RM$50. As these gifts become more the norm and the expectation, the amount of money needed for the *gubahan* increases. Marriage expenses are further increasing as feasts become more elaborate. With just a few exceptions, people still decide to have a traditional feast, often involving more than 1,000 guests.

Children's education is another new expenditure. A generation ago, most people had only a few years of education; now, stopping after six years of primary school is considered premature. Schools are public and free, but there are many expenses associated with sending children to school: uniforms, books and supplies, transportation to and from the school, and money for a daily snack. Some parents pay for extra tutoring or other classes so that their children can perform better on the exams held at the end of Forms 3 and 5 (the equivalent of ninth and eleventh grades in the United States), the successful completion of which is required for advancement in the educational system.

The economic pressures are further exacerbated by the fact that the income derived from fishing does not increase proportionately with years of experience. A fisherman who has recently married for the first time will most likely be making enough to support his family. After ten years of marriage and six children, however, his expenses will have multiplied greatly even though his income will have increased only slightly. The income obtained from fishing does not increase proportionately as people's needs increase as they go through different life stages.

All these cash needs compel a fisherman to stretch his income as far as possible. An income from the traditional ways of catching fish is no longer enough. Younger fishermen are looking wistfully at the larger vessels. More fishermen may consider working on the larger boats as hired hands. But many opt out of fishing altogether. One man is now a truck driver even though he does not like the job; he has a wife and six small children and his fisherman's income did not go far enough. Even if men already working as fishermen are not themselves opting out of fishing, they are encouraging their sons to find other work, which usually requires providing them with more schooling, which in turn increases household expenditures.

The worldview of the people in the community is changing with the globalization of the local economy, especially with regard to the value and prestige attached to specific occupations and the increasingly conservative Islamic rhetoric about men's responsibilities in the household. Both federal and state governments have promoted comprehensive development with the aim of making Malaysia a fully developed country by the year 2020. This campaign, started by Prime Minister Mahathir, is known as Vision 2020. "Vision 2020" has become a pervasive catchphrase. It is seen on billboards and there is a countdown of the days on the front page of a Malay newspaper. It is heard in politicians' speeches as well as in everyday discourse as a shorthand way of justifying someone's economic choices. The future promoted by the Vision 2020 campaign is one of a fully industrialized economy with men and women going to work in factories and living with a high level of material consumption. Nowhere in this picture is there room for the quiet, not-by-the-clock, materially simple existence of the fishermen. As many bright children attend vocational schools and universities, there is a concomitant belief that the men who become fishermen are those who are not smart enough to do anything else. The skills that are required to be a good fisherman and earn the respect of one's community are downplayed, ignored, and treated with contempt by outsiders.

Fishermen themselves have internalized the negative attitudes toward fishing. One man admitted that he stopped fishing to work in a sawmill, even though the income is lower, because his wife thinks that fishing is dirty. Nevertheless, I have seen this same man covered from head to foot with mud after a day's work at the sawmill; I have never seen a fisherman similarly befouled. A certain boat owner also claimed that fishing is dirty, which is why he stays on shore while having someone else operate his boat.

Changing perceptions and expectations are working against the fishermen in other ways, such as gender roles. Fishermen traditionally handed their earnings over to their wives, keeping a portion for themselves to spend as they liked. Revivalist Islamic rhetoric emphasizes the role of the husband and father as head of the household and manager of the household finances. Women in this community have been able to work outside the home in factories or small businesses, and it has been considered appropriate for them to contribute to the household income. Revivalist Islam, however, asserts that husbands are the "rational thinkers" in the household and should be financially responsible for the family. In the ideal, a Muslim husband and father should provide for his family. A man who, during a time of shortfalls, must depend on his wife's ability to supplement household income is falling short of his duty as a Muslim. To pursue an occupation that necessarily involves periodic shortfalls is to choose an option that challenges a man's sense of pride as redefined in the revivalist movement. Malay men do represent their families in the public arena, and leadership within the community tends to be vested in the men. As fishing plays a less prominent role in the community, the skill of a fisherman is considered less important, whereas the household's ability to maintain a desired standard of living gives a man respect in the family as well as in the community.

CONCLUSION

This case study illustrates the ways in which the global economy is threatening the local fishing economy. Part of the threat comes from the management of the marine resources in ways that seek to balance sustainability with fishermen's needs. A much bigger threat, however, comes from the changing needs of the fishermen as they increasingly become part of the market economy. The global economy alters the worldview, including the notions of desirable forms of employment, material culture, and gender relations. The inability to meet the new demands and the low value placed on fishing as an occupation is leading to a gradual demise of the traditional fishing economy in this Malay community.

NOTES

1. The author thanks Thomas Collins, John Wingard, and Satish Kedia for their review of this article and for their helpful comments.
2. This research was made possible by a Fulbright Fellowship and a National Science Foundation Dissertation Improvement Grant.
3. The Fishermen's Subsidy Scheme was started in 1972 for the states on the east coast of Malaysia. The government increased its subsidies in 1981, but then cut the monies available starting in the mid-1980s because of overfishing. At the same time, the government was embarking on an austerity program (Jomo 1991).
4. Personal communication.
5. At the time of research RM$2.5=US$1.

REFERENCES

Aziz, U. A. 1959. *Ekonomi dan Kemiskinan.* Singapore: Pustaka Melayu.
Balakrishnan, N. 1989. The Next NIC. *Far Eastern Economic Review* 145(36):96–98.
Firth, R. 1966. *Malay Fishermen: Their Peasant Economy.* Hamden, Conn.: Archon Books.
Jomo, K. S. 1991. *Fishing for Trouble: Malaysian Fisheries, Sustainable Development, and Inequality.* Kuala Lumpur: Institute for Advanced Studies, University of Malaysia.
———. 1993. Introduction. In *Industrializing Malaysia: Policy, Performance, Prospects,* ed. K. S. Jomo, pp. 1–13. London: Routledge.
Mahathir, M. 1991. Malaysia: The Way Forward. Paper presented at the meeting of the Malaysian Business Council, Kuala Lumpur.
Netting, R. M., R. R. Wilk, and E. J. Arnould, eds. 1984. *Households: Comparative and Historical Studies of the Domestic Group.* Berkeley: University of California Press.
Smith, J. 1984. Nonwage Labor and Subsistence. In *Households and World Economy,* ed. J. Smith, I. Wallerstein, and H-D Evers, pp. 64–69. Beverly Hills, Calif.: Sage.
Tsuruoka, D. 1992. Switch to Industry: Government Sets the Scene for Continued High Growth. *Far Eastern Economic Review* 157(8):66–70.

Grassroots Development Strategies in the Azuero Peninsula of Panama

John R. Bort and James C. Sabella

The economic landscape is rapidly changing as the pace of globalization accelerates throughout the world. Proponents of these changes believe that the unfettered expansion of transnational capitalism heralds a benefi-cent "new world order" (Barnet and Cavanagh 1994; Brecher and Costello 1994). Corporate executives, politicians, economists, and international bankers all extol the virtues of the free market and the benefits of global-ization. For the initiates it is an article of faith that all will materially gain from the North American Free Trade Agreement (NAFTA) and the Gen-eral Agreement on Tariffs and Trade (GATT) (Brown 1993; Earth Island Press 1993). The rewards, however, are usually siphoned off by multina-tional corporations and by the powerful, wealthy, and well connected (Raghavan 1990; Phillips 1991; Bello, Cunningham, and Rau 1994; Rich 1994). For ordinary citizens in most countries of the world, globalization has led neither to greater prosperity nor to an improved standard of living. Their "rewards" are too often diminished job security, rising unemploy-ment, mass layoffs, declines in public services, falling incomes, loss of control over resources, and accelerated environmental degradation (Mead 1991; Daly and Cobb 1994; Danaher 1994). Far from improving the gen-eral lot of humanity, globalization triggers a downward spiral, as the ma-jority slip toward the lowest rungs on the economic ladder (Robinson 1993). The alternative is to promote sustainable development (Lebel and Hal 1989), which focuses on real human beings who are striving to meet their material needs and improve their quality of life (Trzyna 1995). It is axi-omatic that sustainable development should not lead to the impoverish-ment of one group as an acceptable cost of making another group wealthy. Moreover, human needs must be satisfied without severely degrading or destroying the environment (Daly and Cobb 1994; Goodland 1995).

In its present configuration, globalization cannot fulfill the aspirations of the many. Particularly in rural areas of the Third World, corporate-dominated globalization is no more likely to produce lasting benefits than did a host of earlier development initiatives sponsored by a variety of nations and international agencies over the past forty years. In fact, the effects of globalization are far worse, because it has accelerated ecological destruction in regions that once were blessed with an abundance of natural resources (Broad and Cavanagh 1993). For communities whose way of life hinges on maintaining the viability of an ecosystem, such changes can be devastating. There can be no "development" when the ecological underpinnings of an economy are destroyed or so severely degraded that the ecosystem can no longer support the livelihood of its residents.

As David Korten (1995:307) states, "There are few rights more fundamental than the right of people to create caring, sustainable communities and to control their own resources, economies, and means of livelihood." This assertion focuses attention on what is at stake as the wave of economic globalization rolls across local communities. Whose interests will be served in the struggle with the forces unleashed by the race toward economic globalization? This question clarifies the dilemma faced by communities worldwide. Aquaculture, specifically shrimp cultivation, starkly illustrates the problems confronting small communities as the forces of economic globalization reach into ever more remote rural areas.

THE "BLUE REVOLUTION": SHRIMP AQUACULTURE AND GRASSROOTS DEVELOPMENT

Recent studies of shrimp aquaculture in various parts of the world have raised a number of issues related to assessing the impacts of this industry. First, shrimp aquaculture does not really fit into the "blue revolution" model, which is usually described as a grassroots system of production designed to benefit local communities by providing alternative sources of employment and by increasing the availability of animal protein at an affordable price (Weeks and Pollnac 1992). Shrimp is a high-priced export commodity more likely to be associated with intensive, highly capitalized systems of production than with locally controlled, small-scale operations with low capital requirements.

Second, the sustainability of shrimp aquaculture is highly problematic.

Evidence suggests that intensive and semi-intensive production systems are viable for only five to ten years, so new areas for production must be developed as old ones are abandoned. This pattern is illustrated by the experience of the world's top four shrimp-producing countries. In 1994 alone, each abandoned significant areas of shrimp ponds: Thailand 11,000 hectares, Ecuador 2,300 hectares, Indonesia 800 hectares, and India 600 hectares (Calculating Abandonment Rates 1996). It is estimated that 150,000 hectares worldwide were abandoned between 1985 and 1995. Excessive nutrient loading, groundwater depletion, generalized environmental degradation, and the proliferation of diseases have all contributed to breakdowns within segments of these systems (Gujja and Finger-Stich 1996). One must conclude from such overwhelming evidence that monocrop shrimp aquaculture is inherently unstable as presently practiced and that short-term economic benefits may be far outweighed by significant ecosystem costs (Larrson, Folke, and Kautsky 1994).

Third, substantial economic benefits to local communities simply have not materialized. Intensive and semi-intensive methods (1,000–2,000 kilograms/hectare) are far more productive than small-scale traditional methods (100–500 kilograms/hectare), but they are not labor-intensive. Employment rates average only one individual per hectare on the farm and one individual per metric ton off the farm (Gujja and Finger-Stich 1996). Relatively few local individuals are employed, and they can usually find only sporadic, low-paying positions. Since the product is for export, the most significant economic benefits occur well beyond the local community. Moreover, the negative ecological impacts that often accompany these operations may disrupt the other productive enterprises of community members and thereby jeopardize their present standard of living.

THE AZUERO PENINSULA OF PANAMA: GEOGRAPHY

Our case study focuses on Playa (pseudonym), a community on the Bay of Parita on the east side of the Azuero Peninsula. The Azuero, Panama's largest peninsula, juts south into the Pacific Ocean. The topography of the area encompasses a low, flat coastal plain dominated by mangroves and tidal salt flats, rolling hills, and mountains running from northwest to southeast. Its east coast is the driest region in Panama, although rainfall increases toward the south and west. The entire peninsula experiences an intense dry season lasting four or five months, a pattern characteristic of the entire Pacific side of the isthmus (West and Augelli 1989). The coastal area on the eastern side (the provinces of Coclé, Herrera, and Los Santos) has become the center of Panama's shrimp aquaculture industry, which produces about 5,500 metric tons per year (Weidner et al. 1992:617).

HISTORICAL CONTEXT

The region is dotted with many small communities that date to the sixteenth and seventeenth centuries. Throughout most of its history, the area has been relatively isolated in spite of its early settlement. Well into this century, overland contact with Panama City was over crude trails and rough, at times impassable roads. In fact, contact between the larger settlements on the peninsula and Panama City was typically by ship. Throughout the colonial period, the region was essentially a backwater of little interest to the Spanish crown. The region was ignored because the native population disappeared very shortly after the conquest and it had no significant mineral wealth.

The rural population remained relatively isolated and little influenced by external forces. The rural *campesino* population lived in dispersed *ranchos* or in small, close-knit communities that depended on small-scale subsistence agriculture, animal husbandry, and fishing. Small quantities of grain, dried fish, and an occasional cow or chicken were sold to provide cash for the purchase of manufactured goods. The population remained marginal to the commercial economy of Panama well into this century. The region was a world apart from the "transit zone" area around Panama City (West and Augelli 1989).

THE PROBLEM OF FLUCTUATION

The people in the small, traditional coastal communities have had to cope with the raid globalization of the local economy over the past several decades. The most significant changes have been the advent and rapid expansion of export-oriented fishing, shrimp aquaculture, and dry season (January to April) irrigated production of melons for international export.

Activities in the community of Playa will illustrate the strategies used to meet both traditional challenges and changes caused by impinging global forces. Playa has been monitored ethnographically for over a decade and a half, during which time detailed personal histories have been developed for members of extended families. These data illustrate the individual and collective adaptive strategies employed in the community.

Most individuals are frequently involved in a combination of economic activities and also have changed activities at various times. To a casual observer, community members appear to be engaged in a bewildering and chaotic assortment of activities that seem to occur almost randomly. To understand the adaptational patterns of the residents of Playa, it is essential to examine the environmental factors to which they are adapting, as well as the fundamental goals of the individuals living in this area.

Coping with Natural Forces

Marine and terrestrial physical and biological influences can best be described as fluctuating dramatically, rapidly, and unpredictably. Marine resources vary in a predictable seasonal manner, but they are very unpredictable from year to year or over longer periods. For example, scallops became extremely abundant in 1985 and 1986, and large commercial quantities were landed. They have not returned since. Staple resources, such as shrimp, corvina, or snapper, may be abundant in one year and all but disappear the next. The pattern of fluctuation cannot be predicted. To cope with this problem, fishermen use boats and fishing gear that have the versatility to allow for very rapid and relatively inexpensive switching among species and fishing methods.[1]

Fluctuation in agricultural production also requires flexibility. The amount of rainfall varies substantially from year to year. In dry years, less than 1,000 millimeters of rain may fall, causing acute drought conditions. In other years, there may be early rains that allow seeds to germinate, but then a long dry period will follow, causing plants to wither and die. In addition, the Azuero typically experiences a very uneven geographical distribution of rainfall, such that accumulation of water can vary greatly over short distances.

When conditions are optimal, good harvests are possible. When they are not, total crop failure can occur. It is expected that one in three or four crops will either fail completely or produce a marginal harvest. Some individuals elect not to plant at all when the dry season persists or if there is a very late onset of rains, since this pattern is often the harbinger of a short rainy season followed by drought and crop failure. Community members deal with the highly variable rainfall pattern by planting a variety of crops in diverse locations. The people hope that poor harvests in one area will be offset by better conditions in nearby locations.

Raising cattle, the primary livestock animal in the area, presents similar problems. The owner of cattle must decide how many animals to keep through the dry season and how many to sell before it begins. It is extremely risky to maintain large herds with the expectation of a short dry season. In years when the dry season is prolonged, many cattle starve to death as the region's pastures become exhausted. Even if a buyer can be found under such circumstances, the prices will be very low because everyone in the area will also be trying to sell off animals in poor condition as quickly as possible.

Coping with Social and Economic Hazards

National and international economic forces can be even more volatile than natural ones. Fish and shrimp are major sources of income in the area, and markets for them are notoriously unstable. The prices paid for fish in the national market can fluctuate unpredictably in response to supply. For example, if production is high in several areas of the country, the relatively small national market quickly becomes glutted, thus driving down prices.[2]

Equally severe market fluctuations can occur with prime export species such as red snapper or grouper. Large Mexican catches entering the United States, the principal market for Panamanian fish, can depress prices by half in one week. Fresh fish that would have been sent to Miami end up being frozen for later sale The frozen product commands only about half the price of fresh fish.

Coping with Political Instability

Panama's political environment can also be volatile, as was clearly illustrated when Manuel Noriega was deposed. One resident of Playa lost twenty hogs that were en route to market when the U.S. military action began; they simply disappeared in the ensuing chaos. Valuable shipments of fish and shrimp either spoiled or disappeared. For nearly six months after the fall of Noriega's government, the national economy was in shambles. People were out of jobs, and markets were disrupted.

In response, many people of the Azuero reverted to a subsistence economy reminiscent of the past. Activities were almost exclusively oriented toward local subsistence consumption instead of external markets.

The collapse of Panama's government demonstrates the remarkable resiliency of the local population. They coped with the turmoil extremely well, exhibiting none of the violence and economic breakdown that afflicted the cities. In less troubled times, the community has always had to deal with unpredictable or (as the locals believed) capricious government decisions, such as the timing of the closed season *(veda)* on shrimps, or modifications of the legal mesh sizes on fishing nets. The enforcement of fisheries laws is also viewed as well beyond local control. Large shrimp trawlers blatantly violate laws that prohibit them from fishing nearshore waters. Some purse-seiners have permits to take industrial species for fish meal, but they may illegally take and sell large quantities of other species. The widely held view, which is probably justified, is that the rich and the powerful can manipulate the political system to their advantage. The people of Playa deal with this situation simply as another vagary of their environment, and they have learned to cope with it.

PATTERNS OF ADAPTATION

This brief sketch of the uncertainties faced by the people of Playa clarifies the pattern of economic activities and the importance of kinship ties in the community. Nearly everyone is involved in more than one economic pursuit, and there is extensive daily collaboration among kinfolk.

The key to coping with uncertainty in Playa is diversification. Because they engage in a range of activities, the people reduce the impact of problems in any one endeavor. The mix of activities of one individual illustrates this point. He is a part-time watchman who repairs outboard motors, raises pigs, and plants crops in three locations. He also keeps chickens, ducks, rabbits, and turkeys. Most of the crops are for household consumption. Pigs are sold, but the other livestock are for home use. The watchman's job and motor repair bring in a modest cash income. Other individuals combine other activities, but such occupational plurality is typical of the community.

Any single economic activity requires only modest resources. Switching activities can be accomplished with comparative ease when opportunities present themselves, which is an important consideration in this highly variable environment. Individual work histories also indicate that the mix of activities typically changes over time.[3] The individual noted above has fished, worked at other part-time jobs, and varied his mix of crops and livestock, a pattern that is typical throughout the community.

The second buffering mechanism is a strong kinship network. It is an important and mutually beneficial support system. For someone accustomed to neolocal nuclear families, it is often difficult to define the boundaries of a "household" or "domestic unit." Individuals often move from one household to another, and it is not uncommon to find that a person may sleep in one house and eat meals in another—or even at several different houses. Such arrangements are adjustments to available resources and changing needs. What is operating is an extended family system. For example, an unmarried man may have his laundry washed by his sister. The man in turn will provide fish to several related households where he eats at different times, as well as to his sister. If he does not go fishing for a while, a cousin may provide fish. The man may also be helping the cousin's family plant crops or repair nets. The permutations of mutual assistance reinforce the kin-based network.

These ties engender a sense of Playa being the core of an individual's social universe. Residents strongly identify with the community. This solidarity even extends to kin now living beyond its geographical boundaries. They were raised in Playa, and it is the focus of their social network. They commute to Playa nearly every day and participate in the mutual assistance system. With this extended network of social ties, it is easy to understand why members view Playa as a safe haven in an otherwise insecure world. Playa's residents will evaluate any new activity in terms of its possible impact on a wide range of social ties. If a potential change endangers or is potentially disruptive to the social network, it will probably be approached with great caution.

THE DEVELOPMENT OF SHRIMP AQUACULTURE

The impetus for aquacultural development in Playa came from the success of the shrimp fishery. Wild shrimp became a very valuable resource in the Azuero as Panama's shrimp exports boomed in the 1970s in response to escalating international demand. Fishermen were paid $4 or more per pound at the dock.[4] During the heyday of shrimping, men could sometimes earn $75–100 per day. Individual earnings from the wild shrimp fishery fell precipitously as more and more fishermen were drawn to the area by the promise of lucrative returns.[5] By the mid-1980s, fish-ing pressure was so great that many fishermen simply gave up shrimping because the value of the catch often failed to cover their costs of opera-tion. The bonanza was over, at which point some of the residents of Playa decided that they could continue to benefit from the shrimp export industry by raising shrimp.

The idea for a community-based aquaculture venture was stimulated by the Ralston-Purina Company's pioneer shrimp aquaculture program at its Agromarina facility in Aguadulce, a nearby community. Shrimp were raised commercially at Agromarina in a sophisticated system of impoundments into which water was pumped (McCoy 1979). The ex-ample provided by that operation was viewed as a possible addition to fishing and other economic activities. In 1981 several residents of Playa began investigating their options. It was obvious to them that the elabo-rate and expensive system of water pumps and multiple tanks used at the semi-intensive Agromarina facility was far beyond their economic and technical capabilities, although it was thought that it might be possible to raise shrimp using simpler methods.[6]

Community members were thoroughly familiar with the operation of evaporative impoundments, which have long been used to produce salt in the dry season. These structures are set up in low-lying flats (*albinas*) that flood naturally several times per month on high tides. The sea water carries larval and juvenile shrimp into these impoundments. The shrimp that are trapped in the ponds during the rainy season grow rapidly as they feed on algae in the brackish mix of sea and rain water. Once they attain an appropriate size, they are caught with cast nets. The shrimp ponds envisioned in Playa were based on the observation of this annual phenomenon.

The elegantly simply idea for shrimp aquaculture was to construct a low-walled tank with sluice gates within the *albinas*. On flood tides, the gates would be opened to admit water channeled to the tank through ditchlike canals, and then the water would be retained by closing the gates as the tides receded.[7] The walls of the tank could be constructed of earth, and the water control gates could be built with an arrangement of remov-able wooden planks set in a concrete framework. In short, the basic design was simple and relatively inexpensive to construct; it is based on natural tidal flow for water circulation rather than on costly diesel pumps. The Playa approach to aquaculture is one of low input, low capital investment, minimal maintenance, and rudimentary technology.

It is, moreover, important to note that the salt flats most suitable for shrimp aquaculture were available. The best areas for aquaculture bordered on the fringing mangroves and were considered to be wastelands (Macintosh 1982), since they were flooded too frequently to be useful as evaporative ponds. These barren areas are also useless for agriculture or animal husbandry.

Legal and financial questions were examined along with the technical aspects of shrimp cultivation. Arrangements were made to form a legally recognized cooperative, secure the exclusive use of a nearby *albina,* obtain a bank loan, and have a shrimp tank dredged. After two years of discussion, investigation, planning, and preparation, a tank was completed in 1983. A second tank was constructed in 1984.

OPPORTUNISTIC CHANGE

The development and operation of the cooperative was by no means without trouble. From its inception in 1982 until its dissolution in 1987, disagreements arose at virtually every stage. There were perennial tensions over the relative contributions of the thirty-one members of the cooperative. Some members frequently failed to do a fair share of the work required to maintain and operate the tanks. By 1986, membership had declined to twenty-six individuals, although progress continued to be made and a stable, long-term, ecologically sound enterprise was established.

In 1987 matters took a surprising turn. The shrimp tanks were sold and the cooperative was disbanded. The members of the cooperative derived a modest net profit of $300 each from the sale, but the combination of continuing tensions among the members and the potential for a profit became too tempting for some of them to resist. A large minority did not wish to sell the venture, and they held out until the end. Those who did not want to sell formed the core of a second cooperative, which they had established in 1986 to sponsor the construction of two new tanks in another nearby *albina.* These tanks were sold to the same buyer three years later. Similar patterns have emerged in other communities as small-scale aquaculturalists seize the opportunity to sell to highly capitalized entrepreneurs. Since the residents of Playa sold their tanks, the potential of aquaculture has been widely recognized and large expanses of ponds have been developed in the remaining *albinas,* primarily by well-capitalized companies. Grassroots aquaculture appears to have ended.

Even without organizational difficulties, the prospects of local populations retaining control of aquacultural enterprises was problematic from the outset. Local entrepreneurs were initially able to obtain control of the *albinas* because the land was viewed as worthless, rather than as a valuable resource. As the potential for aquaculture was recognized, individuals with more substantial economic resources and better access to technical expertise were attracted to the industry. It was only a matter of time until offers of purchase became too attractive to pass up, and Playa's cooperative experiments in shrimp farming came to an end.

Even though the cooperatives sold out, their experiences provided a valuable glimpse at the potential for sustainable grassroots development. In the final analysis, the problem was probably with the organization of the cooperatives rather than with the aquacultural venture itself. The cooperatives were community-based, a model favored and encouraged by the central government. An alternative model for Playa might focus on kinship-based organizations following traditional patterns of cooperation. Former members of the cooperatives repeatedly expressed the view that cooperatives simply do not work in communities like Playa. We, however, speculate that the flaw may be structural. There are inherent conflicts between the demands of the complex economic relationships among kinfolk and the demands of participation in cooperative activities. Kinship-based obligations take precedence. A better alternative might be to form cooperative organizations along the lines of extended families. Such ventures would more closely parallel the existing system than do those operating on a government-imposed model.[8]

CURRENT TRENDS

The short-term future for aquaculture in the area bordering the Bay of Parita is promising. The area has extensive *albinas* suitable for aquaculture because they can be flooded by natural tidal flow supplemented with artificial pumping. Because of the favorable environmental circumstances, the level of capital investment to establish a viable enterprise has been relatively modest. The comparatively low levels of needed investment tended to stimulate the rapid development of aquaculture in the early 1980s. Expansion was slowed by the economic and political turmoil in Panama in the late 1980s and early 1990s. This situation has changed as Panama's economy has begun recovering and the political conditions have improved. Entrepreneurs are once again seeking areas for profitable investment, and the *albinas* are filling up rapidly as new tanks proliferate.

The shrimp tanks in the area appear to represent only a minimal threat to the local environment; however, this situation could change as the area exploited expands. The *albinas* are separated from the sea by a band of fringing mangroves bisected by rivers and smaller streams. The mangroves, the wide intertidal zone, and the lower river courses that are influenced by tidal flow constitute a very dynamic, productive, and delicately balanced ecosystem. These areas are critical as nurseries for many marine species. Thus far, shrimp aquaculture has not damaged many mangroves, nor has there been major disruption of natural tidal flow or other adverse environmental impacts such as those which have afflicted Taiwan, Ecuador, and Thailand. If expansion continues, however, mangroves are likely to be cut, tidal waters will be redirected, and more estuarine water and groundwater will be pumped into shrimp tanks. These activities could change critical habitats in detrimental ways.

IMPLICATIONS

Playa has been fortunate thus far because the social, economic, and ecological impacts of aquaculture have been minimal or even moderately beneficial. The venture has provided a few full-time jobs as well as occasional work opportunities in shrimp processing. No significant discernible detrimental impacts have occurred to date.[9] This situation is in no small measure due to the extensive *albinas* in the region, which are ideal for shrimp farming but useless for any other purpose. It also appears that present conditions may have the potential for being sustained, barring biological problems such as an uncontrollable outbreak of the tauro virus or another shrimp disease, which can devastate shrimp farms. Most farms still use production methods that present far fewer environmental problems than those associated with more intensive production regimens. Nevertheless, if the limits to aquacultural expansion on the *albinas* are reached and cultivation is expanded geographically, or if more intensive cultivation techniques are implemented, then the present benign situation could change very quickly.[10]

The heart of the industry is currently located in the adjacent provinces of Los Santos and Herrera, where Playa is located. Herrera has about 3,800 hectares of ponds while Los Santos has about 1,700 hectares. Very few areas of open *albina* remain to be developed. Continued geographic expansion presents a significant threat.[11] The present area used for cultivation is expanding at 200 to 300 hectares per year and possibly faster. Estimates range from 7,500 to 12,000 hectares of land suitable for aquacultural development in the entire Republic of Panama, including both *albinas* and mangroves (Weidner et al. 1992:601–2).

If geographic expansion continues, areas of mangrove will have to be cleared to make way for new shrimp ponds, a development that could be catastrophic for the local community because of the critical role that mangroves play as a nursery area for marine life. Loss of mangroves would threaten the existing wild fisheries, and fishermen would lose an extremely important component of their livelihood, as jobs in seafood processing and marketing would also be lost. Even the good local diet, which depends heavily on seafood, would be threatened.

CONCLUSIONS

The critical issue for the future is whether or not the long-term health of the environment and the well-being of the people living in the area will be sacrificed for the short-term profits that can be realized from shrimp cultivation for export. The issue will probably be decided by a combination of factors external to the region. International demand is the force driving the wild shrimp fishery and the expansion of aquaculture. Relatively few of the shrimp produced in Panama are consumed in the country.

Shrimp prices have been relatively stable in the recent past, due in part to the global expansion of aquaculture. The pattern of rapid abandonment of shrimp farms in other regions is continuing, however, and as many as one million hectares may already have been lost to production (Hagler 1997b).[12] As production declines in other areas, it could lead to global price increases, which would in turn increase pressure for expansion in Panama.

The second major consideration will be how issues of conservation and economic development are addressed in the future at the national level. Shrimp is Panama's second largest export, accounting for 11 percent of the country's annual exports of $565 million (USDS 1997). The central government sponsors aquacultural research programs as well as hatchery facilities to produce larval shrimp to be stocked in aquacultural ponds. The intent is obviously to promote the industry. These efforts may contribute to the success of the industry and help preserve the wild fishery by conserving wild larval stocks. At the same time, pressure may be generated to expand the industry by improving shrimp cultivation techniques, making aquaculture even more profitable. Policymakers will certainly be tempted to allow lucrative short-term development with an immediate economic payoff, since the long-term environmental and social costs will not be manifest until they are out of office.[13]

The best hope is that the disastrous experiences in other regions will encourage the exercise of caution and an orientation toward long-term sustainable production that can serve both national and local interests.

NOTES

1. Fishing strategies are considered in more detail in Sabella and Bort (1991) and Bort and Sabella (1989).

2. When markets become saturated, prices can be cut in half from one day to the next and it becomes very difficult even to find buyers.

3. Individual life histories also indicate long-term changes in activity patterns as people age. Men often retire from the rigors of fishing and undertake a less demanding mix of activities, such as marketing, net repair, and the salting of fish.

4. Prices reached $4.75 to $5.25 per pound in the early 1980s and declined to around $4 in the late 1980s. They have remained at that level ever since.

5. During the 1960s and 1970s, the number of individuals involved in fishing in the Playa area increased dramatically from approximately twenty in 1960 to about 400 by the early 1980s. Virtually all of these fishermen were attracted by the opportunities presented by the expanding shrimp fishery. The spectacular catches possible during the early expansion of the fishery no longer occur, as the finite wild shrimp stocks are divided among more and more fishermen.

6. The admittedly imprecise terms "extensive," "semi-intensive," and "intensive" all indicate levels of inputs in aquacultural operation. Extensive systems use little or no pumping of water into tanks, and they rely on natural or slightly enhanced algae growth to feed the shrimp. Semi-intensive and intensive systems employ artificial feed and increasingly sophisticated water circulation systems to sustain higher densities of shrimp in ponds or tanks.

7. The tidal range in the area is about twenty feet, producing a very strong flushing action in properly situated shrimp tanks.

8. Pollnac (1985, 1987), Poggie (1980), and Poggie and Pollnac (1991) have done extensive research on the importance of social and psychological considerations in development efforts in small coastal communities.

9. A few tanks have caused minor flooding of some marginal agricultural land because of their particular placement; it was not seen as a generalized problem.

10. More intensive cultivation systems in other areas have not proven to be sustainable. They are biologically and environmentally unstable and collapse in five to ten years (Calculating Abandonment Rates 1996). Land is used and then abandoned when aquaculture is no longer possible. The impact on the local population in this scenario might not be too extreme, assuming that environmental damage does not result from the heavy pumping of water and supplemental feeding associated with intensification. Some jobs would be lost, but traditional economic patterns could continue.

11. The rapid loss of mangroves around the world is alarming, and the FAO (1995) attributes over half of that loss to the development of shrimp aquaculture.

12. Taiwan provides a spectacular and highly publicized illustration of how catastrophically intensive shrimp cultivation systems can collapse. It was the world's largest exporter of cultured shrimp in 1987 at 90,000 metric tons. Exports declined to 25,000 metric tons in 1989 and have remained at that level ever since (Hagler 1997a).

13. A broader overview of shrimp aquacultural development in Central America is provided by Bort, Ovares, and Stonich (1996) and Stonich, Bort, and Ovares (1997).

REFERENCES

Barnet, R. J., and J. Cavanagh. 1994. *Global Dreams: Imperial Corporations and the New World Order.* New York: Simon and Schuster.

Bello, W., S. Cunningham, and B. Rau. 1994. *Dark Victory: The United States, Structural Adjustment and Global Poverty.* Oakland, Calif.: Food First.

Bort, J. R., L. L. Ovares, and S. C. Stonich. 1996. Las Expectativas y Problemas del Desarrollo de la Acuacultura del Camarón en Centroamérica. *Ciencias Ambientales* 12:93–100.

Bort, J. R., and J. C. Sabella. 1989. Appropriate Technology and Autonomous Development Strategies in the Azuero Peninsula of Panama. In *Marine Resource Utilization: Proceedings of a Conference on Social Science Issues,* ed. S. J. Thomas, L. Maril, and E. P. Durrenberger, pp. 50–65. Mobile: University of South Alabama College of Arts and Sciences and the Mississippi–Alabama Sea Grant Consortium.

Brecher, J., and T. Costello. 1994. *Global Village or Global Pillage: Economic Reconstruction from the Bottom Up.* Boston: South End Press.

Broad, R., and J. Cavanagh. 1993. *Plundering Paradise: The Struggle for the Environment in the Philippines.* Berkeley: University of California Press.

Brown, M. B. 1993. *Fair Trade: Reform and Realities in the International Trading System.* London: Zed.

Calculating Abandonment Rates. 1996. *Environment* 38(7):36.

Daly, H. E., and J. B. Cobb. 1994. *For the Common Good: Redirecting the Economy toward Community, the Environment, and a Sustainable Future.* 2d ed. Boston: Beacon Press.

Danaher, K., ed. 1994. *Fifty Years Is Enough: The Case against the World Bank and the International Monetary Fund.* Boston: South End Press.

Earth Island Press. 1993. *The Case against Free Trade: GATT, NAFTA, and the Globalization of Corporate Power.* San Francisco: Earth Island Press.

Food and Agricultural Organization (FAO). 1995. *World Fisheries: Problems and Prospects.* Rome: FAO Committee on Fisheries.

Goodland, R. 1995. *Environmental Sustainability: Universal and Rigorous.* Washington, D.C.: World Bank Environmental Department.

Gujja, B., and A. Finger-Stich. 1996. What Price Prawn? Shrimp Aquaculture's Impact on Asia. *Environment* 38(7):12–32.

Hagler, M. 1997a. *The Environmental Damage Caused by Shrimp Farming.* http://www.greenpeaceusa.org/reports/biodiversity/shrimp/shrimp03.

———. 1997b. *Shrimp Farming: Production and Consumption.* http://www.greenpeaceusa.org/reports/biodiversity/shrimp/shrmp03.html#farmed.

Korten, D. C. 1995. *When Corporations Rule the World.* West Hartford, Conn.: Kumarian Press.

Larrson, J., C. Folke, and N. Kautsky. 1994. Ecological Limitations and Appropriations of Ecosystem Support by Shrimp Farms in Cambodia. *Environmental Management* 18(5):663–76.

Lebel, G. G., and J. Hal. 1989. *Sustainable Development: A Guide to "Our Common Future: The Report of the World Commission on Environment and Development."* Washington, D.C.: Global Tomorrow Coalition.

McCoy, E. 1979. *Feasibility of Pond Aquaculture of Shrimp in Panama.* Panama City: Directorate of Aquaculture, Ministry of Agriculture.

Macintosh, D. J. 1982. Fisheries and Aquaculture: Significance of Mangrove Swamps. In *Recent Advances in Aquaculture,* ed. J. F. Muir and R. J. Roberts, pp. 12–27. Boulder, Colo.: Westview Press.

Mead, W. R. 1991. *The Low-Wage Challenge to Global Growth: The Labor Cost-Productivity Imbalance in Newly Industrializing Countries.* Washington, D.C.: Economic Policy Institute.

Phillips, K. 1991. *The Politics of Rich and Poor.* New York: Harper Perennial.

Poggie, J. J. 1980. Small-Scale Fishermen's Psychocultural Characteristics and Cooperative Formation. *Anthropological Quarterly* 53:18–32.

Poggie, J. J., and R. B. Pollnac. 1991. Community Context and Cooperative Success in Ecuador. In *Small-Scale Fishery Development: Sociocultural Perspectives,* ed. J. J. Poggie and R. B. Pollnac, pp. 1–29. Kingston: International Center for Marine Resource Development, University of Rhode Island.

Pollnac, R. B. 1985. Social and Cultural Characteristics in Small-Scale Fishery Development. In *Putting People First: Sociological Variables in Rural Development,* ed. M. Cernea, pp. 259–300. New York: Oxford University Press.

———. 1987. *People's Participation in Small-Scale Fisheries Development Cycle.* Kingston: International Center for Marine Resource Development, University of Rhode Island.

Raghavan, C. 1990. *Recolonization, GATT, the Uruguay Round, and the Third World.* Penang, Malaysia: Third World Network.

Rich, B. 1994. *Mortgaging the Earth: The World Bank, Environmental Impoverishment, and the Crisis of Development.* Boston: Beacon Press.

Robinson, I. 1993. *North American Trade as If Democracy Mattered: What's Wrong with NAFTA and What Are the Alternatives?* Ottawa: Canadian Center for Policy Alternatives and International Labor Rights Education and Research Fund.

Sabella, J. C., and J. R. Bort. 1991. Navigating Troubled Waters: Survival Strategies of Artisanal Fishermen in Panama and Peru. In *Small-Scale Fishery Development: Sociocultural Perspectives,* ed. J. J. Poggie and R. B. Pollnac, pp. 57–71. Kingston: International Center for Marine Resource Development, University of Rhode Island.

Stonich, S. C., J. R. Bort, and L. L. Ovares. 1997. Globalization of Shrimp Mariculture: The Impact on Social Justice and Environmental Quality in Central America. *Society and Natural Resources* 10:161–79.

Trzyna, T. 1995. *A Sustainable World.* Sacramento, Calif.: International Center for the Environment and Public Policy.

U.S. Department of State (USDS). 1997. *Background Notes: Panama.* http://www.stat-usa.gov/BEN/inqprogs2/webdoc.egi/public/regional/873/panama.

Weeks, P., and R. B. Pollnac. 1992. Introduction: Coastal Aquaculture in Developing Countries—Problems and Perspectives. In *Small-Scale Fishery Development: Sociocultural Perspectives,* ed. J. J. Poggie and R. B. Pollnac, pp. 89–104. Kingston: International Center for Marine Resource Development, University of Rhode Island.

Weidner, D., T. Revord, R. Wells, and A. Manuar. 1992. *World Shrimp Culture: Central America.* Washington, D.C.: U.S. Department of Commerce.

West, R. C., and J. P. Augelli. 1989. *Middle America: Its Lands and Peoples.* Englewood Cliffs, N.J.: Prentice-Hall.

Local Stratagems, Global Spoils: Monopoly Power and Contract Farming in the Belize Banana Industry

Mark Moberg

Among the most significant structural changes to have occurred in tropical agriculture in recent years has been a shift from large-scale plantation production to various forms of subcontracting (Little 1994; Grossman 1998). Such arrangements have been initiated by the multinational corporations that dominate world markets in crops such as bananas, coffee, cacao, citrus, and sugar. Throughout much of Central America, banana multinationals that once directly controlled vast landholdings have sold off many of their fixed assets to private growers. While divesting themselves of many of their farming operations, some of the multinationals that now subcontract production continue to provide the financing and input requirements for their contract partners. Although heralded by the banana multinationals as equal partnerships between independent parties, such arrangements are not without their critics. Nor, for that matter, is subcontracting in tropical agribusiness as novel a relationship as its proponents have claimed. As long ago as 1936, Charles Kepner pointed out in his classic study, *Social Aspects of the Banana Industry,* that subcontracting enabled United Fruit to bolster profits by divesting itself of both agronomic risks and problems of labor recruitment and control.

Since its inception in the early 1970s, the modern banana industry in Belize has remained nominally independent of direct corporate control. The industry was a government-owned entity until 1984; it had been established to boost export revenues and employment opportunities in Stann Creek and Toledo, two economically depressed districts in the southern part of the country.[1] Following implementation of a structural adjustment agreement mandated by the International Monetary Fund in 1984, the state was compelled to privatize the industry, resulting in the division of its holdings among various Belizean and expatriate growers.

All growers in Belize sell their fruit to Fyffes Group, Ltd., Europe's largest banana multinational and a former subsidiary of United Fruit. This arrangement might be considered emblematic of the subcontracting relationships that multinationals have promoted in recent years, but it differs little from Kepner's description of the 1930s. Through a carefully considered combination of intimidation and co-optation, Fyffes has secured an effective monopoly over the Belizean industry by denying farmers access to alternative outlets for their production. By such strategies, the multinational has externalized the costs and risks of banana production to private growers, while setting the prices that growers receive for their fruit.

The twenty-three privately owned farms that now constitute the Belizean banana sector systematically rely on fraud, ethnic discrimination, and threatened violence or deportation as methods of labor control. Such practices pervade banana-producing regions throughout the Americas, as demonstrated by the extensive scholarly and journalistic literature devoted to the banana multinationals and their questionable labor policies. The goal of this article is not to update the litany of abuses associated with Central American plantations for the past century; rather, it is to show how the harsh labor relations on Belizean farms originate in the global strategies of banana multinationals to maintain monopolies over their local suppliers. By dictating ruinous prices and marketing conditions to private growers, Fyffes ultimately structures local working conditions, despite the fact that farms are not under its direct control. Most previous investigators argued that severe working conditions on Central American banana farms are the result of neocolonial or racist attitudes among the North Americans assigned to manage corporate plantations. Yet equally abusive conditions exist on the smaller, locally managed, and privately owned farms that are part of the Belizean industry. We may infer that harsh labor relations are a structural aspect of the global banana trade as it is controlled by a handful of companies. To explicate the origins of abusive working conditions, it is necessary to explain the political and economic structures that connect local farms to the world market; recourse to some autonomous realm of racial discourse or ideology is beside the point.

STRATAGEMS AND SPOILS IN THE WORLD BANANA TRADE

From its very outset, the world banana trade has been dominated by a few large corporations. U.S.-based banana multinationals originated in the railroad and steamship companies that opened the Caribbean coast of Central America between 1870 and 1900. Having gained control of the region's only internal and foreign transportation links, such firms secured instant regional monopolies over the purchase and export of fruit. In the ensuing years, company railroads passed into government hands, but the banana companies closely guarded their control over land and independent growers. By the mid-1930s, the largest of these entities, the United Fruit Company (now known by its popular trademark, Chiquita), directly cultivated only 139,000 acres of land, although it indirectly controlled the "independent" growers on over twenty times that much acreage. Voracious land acquisitions of this sort severely limited the availability of land to the company's would-be competitors (McCann 1976:39–40). United Fruit and its major rivals defended their massive landholdings in terms of their periodic need to relocate production sites due to disease and soil exhaustion. Until the development of disease-resistant varieties in the 1950s, banana plantations faced the constant threat of a soil-borne fungus (*Fusarium cubense,* or Panama disease) that caused widespread production losses. To contend with the disease, the banana companies established widely dispersed plantations of tens of thousands of acres each (known as "divisions"), only to abandon them as each fell prey to infection. With each relocation, the companies "systematically destroyed the infrastructure [they] had constructed (railroads, bridges, telephone lines, etc.) in order to prevent competitors from being able to renew production on a smaller scale" (Bourgois 1989:8).

Disease-resistant varieties have stabilized banana production in Central America since the 1950s, although the multinationals continue to control pricing and defeat strikes by relying on their dispersed operations throughout the hemisphere. Banana workers constitute the most militant sector of organized labor in Central America, and they have staged combative strikes for improved wages and working conditions in Honduras, Costa Rica, and Guatemala (MacCameron 1983; Argueta 1992). Yet even disciplined nationwide strikes have been defeated by the companies' ability to compensate with production from other, nonstriking divisions. Should the strategy of attrition fail, the banana companies have recourse to more direct forms of labor control. Since the 1940s, every United Fruit division has maintained blacklists of "undesirable" employees, a policy that complements even older practices of spying on workers and defeating strikes by importing ethnically distinct strikebreakers (Purcell 1993; Echeverri-Gent 1992). In the early 1980s, the multinationals refined these time-tested practices by transferring their blacklists to a centralized computer database (Bourgois 1989:12).

Much as the companies dictate wages to their field employees, they set prices to their independent suppliers by limiting access to alternative buyers. They do so by temporarily paying higher prices than competitors and even purchasing fruit at a loss until all rivals withdraw from the market. Short-term losses are offset by profits generated in markets where company monopolies are secure. By similar means, the multinationals have thwarted independent marketing efforts among their contract farmers. In the 1930s, Jamaican banana growers organized a cooperative that managed an export operation (including its own shipping line) that was the rival of the one run by United Fruit. Refusing to tolerate a competitor for supplies of Jamaican bananas, United Fruit raised its producer prices far higher than those of the cooperatives to win over many of its independent suppliers. Within two years, the company was able to dictate the terms of surrender in its price war with the Jamaican growers; among other conditions, the company specified that the co-op was to cease exporting fruit to the United States and to pay its members no more than the prices established by United Fruit for Jamaican bananas (Black 1984:77; Holt 1992).

Such strategies account in large part for the remarkably consistent profitability of the banana multinationals, even during depressions and wars that diminished the earnings of other agricultural commodity exporters. Between 1900 and 1951, United Fruit earned an average of 12.5 percent of its net worth each year, and the company's value increased from $12.5 million to $320 million. During the same period, the company never experienced a net loss, and with the exception of one year, it always commanded at least 50 percent of the U.S. market share of bananas (Dosal 1993:6). While seeking to preserve profitable monopolies in each of their spheres of operation, the banana multinationals are engaged in fierce and often extralegal competition over sources of fruit. In theory, competition among multinationals could allow growers to negotiate more favorable marketing arrangements. As will be seen, however, their inability to do so is attributable to the multinationals' efforts to exclude all potential competitors from their areas of expertise.

The world markets are dominated by just five North American and European banana companies.[2] Production processes, producer prices, wages, and working conditions therefore tend everywhere to be driven by decisions taken in a few corporate boardrooms. In Belize, all fruit is purchased and exported by Fyffes Group, Ltd., the largest European banana importer and, until 1986, a fully owned subsidiary of Chiquita. Production processes on private Belizean banana farms are little different from those on the massive corporate plantations of Honduras and Guatemala. Such similarities arise ostensibly from marketing strategies accommodating the tastes of North American and European consumers. Fyffes rejects fruit with any evidence of mishandling, claiming that consumers in the developed countries will not buy such produce. The company also refuses to pay for fruit that falls outside a range between 6.5 and 10 inches in length, or that has fewer than three "fingers" per "hand." Specifications for salable produce result not only in a massive waste of otherwise edible fruit but also provide Fyffes with a powerful mechanism for disciplining its restive suppliers. There is no direct corporate control over the Belizean banana industry, and yet pricing, quality control, and marketing conditions closely influence the wage and working conditions on each farm. The abuses reported on plantations throughout Central America therefore have their local counterparts, largely because such practices are essential to survival in the face of pricing dictates by the banana multinational.

The Belizean industry is distinguishable from the massive United Fruit division documented in Bourgois's pioneering study (1989) by the diversity of farm operations and the variety of local and imported populations put to work on them. The Belizean banana sector consists of twenty-three farms ranging in size from 3 to 200 hectares, with a median size of 72 hectares. Owners of the smallest farms rely on no more labor than that of their immediate families, while their large-scale counterparts may command small armies of 300 or more workers. The largest farms recruit male and female workers of up to four nationalities speaking seven languages. By far the largest single component of the banana workforce consists of relatively recent Central American immigrants. Most of these workers were among the estimated 2 million Central Americans uprooted by the region's civil and economic crises since 1980 (Palacio 1993). By law, immigrant workers in Belize are required to hold government-issued work permits, but a survey of 148 foreign workers on six farms revealed that some 35 percent were undocumented (Moberg 1996c:429).

Of the 1,380 field workers employed on the nation's banana farms in 1993, 34 percent were Guatemalans, 32 percent were Hondurans, and 25 percent were Salvadorans. Working conditions and labor relations in Cowpen, site of the country's four largest farms, have been imported from Central America as well. Most of the managers and field supervisors at Cowpen are immigrants themselves, veterans of Chiquita, Dole, and Del Monte who have transferred to Belize the harsh labor relations that exist on Honduran or Guatemalan farms. As one immigrant worker described his supervisors,

> Ah, yes—they're all Hondurans or Guatemalans, but they treat us like slaves. They all exploit us. Here workers are supposed to earn $18 [US$9] for a nine-hour day, but you won't find any who brings home more than $14 to $16. I know they are supposed to pay time-and-a-half for work over forty-eight hours, but not one farm here pays that. What can we do? If you complain, they fire you on the spot. I know workers who were poisoned when they were spraying Gramoxone [paraquat]. When they asked to be reassigned to do something else, they were fired instead. The managers have plenty here to take your place.

Interviews with other Cowpen workers suggest that these are not isolated claims. "Very oppressive," a captain on another farm described local working conditions. "All the companies have their *orejas* [ears, or informers]. They pay them to report on people that the companies consider troublemakers. That means no one is going to talk about unions or strikes here, because you don't know whether your best friend is getting a little extra to report what he hears."

Underpayment, spying, and summary dismissal are common occurrences at Cowpen, and it is not unusual for workers to go unpaid for prolonged periods. Under Belizean law, farm workers must be paid every two weeks, or *quincena*. Most farms observe these provisions, albeit with the underpayment and deception mentioned above. Two of the Cowpen farms have had a history of mismanagement under the ownership of Danish investors, who subsequently contracted with Fyffes to manage the farms. Even under the new management, the farms continued to skip pay periods due to cash shortages. Other than managers, the workforce on the two farms is composed almost entirely of very recent immigrants, as those farms have acquired a bad reputation among more experienced workers. Some workers surveyed on the Danish-owned farms had gone two months without pay. In the absence of regular wages, workers are forced to purchase their necessities on credit at employer-run stores whose prices exceed those of independent retailers by 30 to 40 percent. Unpaid workers seethe with frustration at their predicament (described by some as slavery), for they fear that if they leave the Danes to work elsewhere, they will never collect their back pay.

Such incidents led the Human Rights Commission of Belize to investigate working conditions on several banana farms. At one, investigators found children extensively employed in the packing shed in violation of the law. While they were held to the same expectations as adult workers, children were paid just 50 percent of the minimum wage. Payroll records were poorly kept, with hours or tasks paid often being substantially less than the amount of work actually performed. Most of the workers in the banana belt are illiterate, and virtually none speak English; as such, they are easily tricked on paydays and have little recourse to English-speaking government officials charged with enforcing labor laws. In the event that workers detect discrepancies in their pay, the presence of armed security guards and a captain wearing a .38-caliber pistol on his belt tends to discourage complaints. A subsequent investigation by the government's Labor Department in 1993 corroborated the Human Rights Commission's findings, leading the government to order several farms to pay back wages of $250,000. The government order notwithstanding, workers on the farms do not report any change in pay procedures.

Although workers on most farms experience periodic abuses, the industry was devoid of organized resistance between the early 1980s and 1995, a period when managers replaced unionized Belizean workers with immigrants (Alonso 1987; Moberg 1996b). The absence of collective resistance among current workers reflects the determination of managers to detect and fire labor organizers before workers are able to mobilize. For the remaining workers, the swift public retribution meted out to those who challenge managerial authority serves as a sobering reminder of their own insecurity. Despite such risks, a clandestine organizing drive in 1995 forced a work stoppage on the Cowpen farms and compelled their owners to schedule negotiations with a newly formed union of banana workers. The promises proved to have been made in bad faith, and before negotiations could take place, the growers had called on the Belizean military to intervene. The organizing drive was abruptly crushed when almost 200 workers were rounded up at gunpoint and trucked to the Guatemalan border for deportation. The use of officially sanctioned force against strikers that is common throughout Central America now occurs in Belize as well, although that country formerly distinguished itself from the rest of the region by its putatively democratic traditions. As a Belizean television reporter commented during the suppression of the strike, "One of the things that disturbed a lot of citizens in Belize City was when they saw the news coverage and saw the Belizean army dressed as if they were in Salvador or Guatemala and carrying big guns. It was difficult to appreciate that we were looking at a section of Belizean society and that this was going on" (Moberg 1997:172–79).

"WE HAVE TO PUNISH YOU": FYFFES AND THE GROWERS

Asked to account for working conditions at Cowpen and other banana farms, owners are defensive but consistent in their explanations. Most of them acknowledge that wages and working conditions are worse on banana farms than in other agricultural sectors, but they frequently observe that their workers are paid more than banana workers in Guatemala or Honduras. Such assertions are nominally true, at least when it comes to the stated wages. But those wages are not always actually paid. Moreover, banana workers in Guatemala and Honduras also receive paid vacations, "thirteenth month" annual bonuses,[3] and company-provided medical care, none of which is found on any Belizean farm. Growers assert that their high costs of production, combined with the low, unpredictable prices paid by Fyffes, simply do not allow them to improve the wages or benefits received by their workers.

Even on small farms, the input expenses of banana production are great. Many expenses are deducted automatically from the box price, so growers see only a small fraction of the producer price when they are paid for a shipment of fruit. From the current base price of Bze$13.08 (US$6.54) per forty-pound box, $4.22 is deducted in levies for the Banana Growers' Association (BGA), export taxes, port use, a disaster insurance fund, and the purchase of boxes from Fyffes at $2 each. An additional $1.30 is deducted from each box by the BGA for aerial spraying to control Black Sigatoka, a fungus that has threatened the country's banana farms in recent years. When wages and farmer-supplied inputs are taken into account, what initially appears to be a profitable crop generates a slim profit of just $1.55 (US$0.78) per box, according to the BGA's own best-case estimate.

All fruit grown on Belizean banana farms is destined for the European Union (EU), where marketing of bananas is governed by a succession of treaties first negotiated in Togo in 1975 and known as the Lomé Convention. Under its terms, bananas from forty-six African, Caribbean, and Pacific (ACP) states that were former European colonies can be imported into the EU free of duty, while all other fruit, notably from the "dollar area" sources of Latin America, are subject to a 20 percent tariff. These levies have not entirely excluded Latin American fruit from Europe, as production costs throughout the dollar area are lower than those for ACP producers. They have, however, acted as market preferences, ensuring that producers in countries such as Belize are able to remain competitive with their counterparts in neighboring countries. Subsequent modifications of the Lomé Convention permitted fruit companies to import one box of dollar area fruit free of duty for every box they import of ACP fruit.

Corporate competition for supplies of fruit is played out against the background of such marketing agreements. Lacking suppliers in the ACP countries, Chiquita, Dole, and Del Monte have been severely affected by EU agreements favoring such sources.[4] For its part, Fyffes has attempted to maintain sources in both ACP and dollar areas in order to import as much fruit as possible free of duty. It has begun importing bananas to Europe from Guatemala and Honduras in addition to its more established sources in Belize, Suriname, and the Dominican Republic. The multinationals jealously guard their sources to limit competition in the prices they pay to private suppliers. As a result, Fyffes's entry into Honduras was systematically blocked by its former parent company, Chiquita, while Del Monte strenuously opposed Fyffes's entry into Guatemala. The result of these rivalries was a series of extralegal corporate skirmishes that Graham Pritchard, Fyffes's representative in Belize, referred to as "banana wars."

In 1988, the first freight train carrying Fyffes bananas to port in Honduras was mysteriously stopped and sidelined; railway officials explained to frantic representatives of the company that it had been "lost." With some cajoling and bribery, Fyffes was able to get the bananas to port, only to confront other obstacles. After the bananas were loaded onto a freighter, Chiquita lawyers obtained a restraining order forcing the ship to unload. With its bananas ripening on the dock, Fyffes sought to override the order. Pritchard explained, "They've got their judges and we've got ours. We had ours issue orders countermanding theirs so that the boats could be loaded again." While such maneuvers failed in the end to stop the shipment, the added transport time and handling of that first cargo left it a near-total loss by the time it reached England. According to Fyffes, its operations in Honduras continue to be entangled in legal obstacles erected by Chiquita.

Such proprietary control of sources is by no means limited to Honduras and Guatemala. In Belize, an ACP country, Fyffes is concerned that the U.S.-based banana multinationals may want to win over its suppliers to obtain preferential access to the European market. A ruddy-faced and usually genial Englishman, Pritchard visibly stiffened when asked to discuss specific aspects of Fyffes's contract with Belizean growers ("How do I know you won't go to work for Dole next year after I provide this information?"). On the other hand, members of the BGA, which represents all of the country's commercial banana producers, readily volunteered the contract information that Fyffes was reluctant to release. When discussing relations between the company and its suppliers, Pritchard asserted that if growers object to their contract with Fyffes, they are free to seek other buyers. "After all," he said, "they are independent parties. They don't have to sell to us."

There is no legal barrier to the entry of Fyffes's corporate rivals into Belize, and many growers privately state that they would welcome the competition provided by Chiquita or Dole. At present, however, Fyffes does all in its power to retain its monopoly over banana exports from Belize. The current contract with Fyffes is an intricate document setting forth in large part the obligations of growers to their marketing partner. Of primary concern to most growers is the determination of fruit prices, for while a base price of Bze$13.08 per forty-pound box is specified in the contract, actual prices paid by Fyffes fluctuate radically according to the quality rating assigned to each farm's shipment. Fyffes imposes penalties on growers for short box weights, overripened fruit, and low quality. All fruit supplied by growers must be free of blemishes, scars more than one inch in length, and discoloration, and no more than two hands per box may consist of three fingers (all other hands must have four or more). Growers are not paid for any fruit that fails to meet these criteria, and yet Fyffes reportedly finds markets for all the fruit that it receives in edible condition, either among retail outlets or institutional buyers.

Scoring is an involved process that directly determines fruit prices, yet to many growers it is a mysterious, if not arbitrary factor affecting their operations. Upon the arrival of each Fyffes shipment in England, the company's quality scorers open a sample of boxes from each farm and evaluate the fruit along thirteen criteria relating to ripeness, scarring, blemishes, rot, width, and length. Each box is scored for the percentage of unblemished fruit, and these percentages are then averaged for the entire sample from that farm. This sample average constitutes the Percent Mean Score (PCMS) of that farm's shipment, which directly determines the price paid to the grower.

In what it describes as an incentive to produce the highest quality fruit, Fyffes pays growers quality bonuses of up to $6 per box above the contract price if fruit is scored at eighty-five PCMS or above. Should the score fall below sixty, however, Fyffes imposes penalties that may result in up to $6 deducted per box. As a result, growers not infrequently owe money to the company after it has ostensibly "purchased" their fruit. On one farm, an inexperienced packing crew packed shorter (6.5–7.5 inch) fruit in forty-pound boxes, instead of in the twenty-eight pound boxes reserved for such fruit. The shipment of seventy-seven boxes was scored at just thirty PCMS, almost entirely because of the error. While the fruit was otherwise of good quality and was undoubtedly sold by Fyffes to retailers, the grower was penalized $980 for the shipment. One-time losses for low quality scores can be substantial, but of greater concern to growers is the company's punitive response to consecutively low scores. The contract specifies that if two shipments from a farm in thirty days fall below a score of sixty, Fyffes will refuse to accept a third shipment from the same farm.

Under these contract conditions, growers assume all the risk of the twenty-one to twenty-three-day transatlantic passage, for their scores and farm receipts suffer if ships are delayed or fruit is damaged in handling. Concerns about fruit quality are particularly acute for Belizean growers, as Fyffes ships make three or four additional port calls in Central America and the Caribbean after leaving Belize. During each of these stops, the ships' refrigerated holds are opened, exposing fruit to high temperature and humidity levels that hasten ripening. Although the issue of quality scoring is raised annually in negotiations with the company, Fyffes has been adamant in its refusal to consider any other system. The BGA attempted to have quality assessed in Belize before ships are loaded and, failing that, to have growers' representatives stationed in England to observe the scoring process. Neither alternative was acceptable to the company, and growers ultimately signed the contract without changes. Several representatives of the BGA claim that scorers have an incentive to grade "hard" because they are rewarded by the company for low scores. Fyffes saves money when fruit receives low grades, and scorers receive bonuses for such savings. More outspoken growers contend that the scoring system is used in a punitive fashion to retaliate

against those growers that Fyffes's local representatives see as too as-
sertive and to intimidate others into acquiescence.

Brian Seals, an outspoken North American grower, claims that most
small farms receive good marks because Fyffes prefers to cultivate its
relations with small growers. The company's bias toward smallholders
in turn affects the BGA's stance toward the company, since the former's
policies are decided on a one-person, one-vote basis. Over five to six
shipments, Seals asserts, any large farm "will take a hit," suffering a
substantial drop in quality assessment. "That way," he claims, "Fyffes
makes sure that only a couple of growers are mad at any one time, and
most are satisfied enough that they won't unite to challenge them." Some
growers allege that these sampling and quality scoring procedures are
the means by which Fyffes guarantees high profits for its shareholders
and bonuses for its executive officers. To its British retailers, Fyffes offers annual wholesale price contracts at a fixed price (about £12 or
US$20 per forty-pound box). "Now how can they offer fixed annual
contracts to retailers on the basis of fluctuating producer prices and production levels?" Seals asked. "I'll tell you how: they set the price to us
by manipulating quality measures. The way they have it arranged now,
it is almost literally impossible for Fyffes not to generate a profit."

In addition to quality scoring provisions and penalties, the contract
specifies growers' obligations concerning the size of shipments. The
growers are collectively required to supply Fyffes with at least 60,000
boxes of fruit every two weeks, all of which must be delivered to the
company within thirty-six hours of harvest. Should the industry fail to
meet this target, the company claims the right to suspend all purchases
in Belize until the level of production improves. The BGA is required to
provide Fyffes with an estimate of the number of boxes to be shipped
eight weeks before the fruit is actually harvested so that the company
can procure a ship of appropriate capacity. This policy enables Fyffes to
hire vessels whose cargo holds will be filled to capacity so as to minimize transport costs per box. If the growers fall short of this estimate by
more than 5 percent, they are charged $7.65 per box for each shortfall,
the penalty being levied against those farms that fail to meet their estimates. The contract, moreover, provides contingencies that insulate Fyffes
against unexpected changes in world market conditions. In the event of
devaluation of the Belizean dollar, for example, Fyffes will consider
renegotiations of prices no sooner than two months after the devaluation, and then only at its option. Finally, Fyffes retains the right to rene-

gotiate any aspect of the contract in the event of unexpected changes in world trade or banana marketing agreements. "Do you see any way," an incredulous BGA official asked after describing these contract conditions, "that Fyffes failed to cover their ass?"

Apart from acting as a purchaser of Belizean bananas, Fyffes has become involved in production on a few farms. This strategy has enabled the company to cultivate alliances with several BGA members, who then side with the company interests in BGA votes. In 1992, Fyffes purchased an 85 percent share of one of the largest grower's farms, which it operates in partnership with him. Fyffes also assumed management of two of the Danish-owned farms, for which it was paid a management fee plus 25 percent of their quality bonuses. Two of the region's small growers were already employed on the Danish farms as supervisors, and they received hefty raises when Fyffes took over management. For those growers who are not beneficiaries of such largesse, however, the company's involvement in production often amounts to unwanted intrusion, if not intimidation. Since 1990, the company has operated a program by which fertilizer and nematicide are made available to growers on interest-free credit. Those growers who have become reliant on such low-cost inputs have been reluctant to criticize the company, for fear of being cut out of the program.

On harvest days, Pritchard and another Fyffes employee visit each of the region's farms to evaluate fruit and make suggestions for farm maintenance. Many growers resent such inspections, which are seen as a particularly humiliating aspect of their relationship with the multinational. Brian Seals recalled one such farm visit, which set the pattern for his subsequent strained relations with the company:

> Once I refused to acquiesce when [Pritchard] "suggested" that we follow some procedures and new input usage on the farm. Now these are supposed to be only suggestions, and I told him, no, we won't do it because it will cost us money and I don't believe we'll see any benefits. That guy actually said to me, "Well, then we're going to have to punish you." I told him if I ever hear him say those words again when he's on my farm, I will physically throw him off.

Fyffes's contract conditions have angered most growers, and a few of them have, at their own initiative, sought more favorable terms from other corporations. Two of the region's largest growers have made clandestine overtures to Chiquita, which is reportedly eager to gain access to an ACP source of fruit. The company indicated a willingness to pay Belizean suppliers up to $19 per box as a base price, with up to $4 per box as a quality bonus. One of the growers announced the results of his discussions with Chiquita at a BGA meeting and urged its members to terminate their contract with Fyffes. The BGA refused to do so, albeit by a narrow vote. That a majority of the members acquiesced to Fyffes may seem astonishing, given the vehement sentiments detailed above. The vote, however, surprised few members of the BGA, which has failed to unite against Fyffes because the company can readily count on allies among those growers to whom it has offered partnerships, credit, and employment. Growers openly admit that some within their ranks enjoy comfortable relationships with the company that vastly diminish their perceived common interests as banana producers. When asked why growers do not seek other marketing arrangements, Brian Seals replied:

> They're scared. Look, Smithson is in with Fyffes. The Danes owe their ass to Fyffes. Castillo and Nuñez have jobs with Fyffes. So anything that's discussed in the BGA immediately gets back to Pritchard. If you go to one of those meetings, it's a farce. Maybe four or five guys do all the talking. Everybody else is scared stiff. What are they scared of? Imagine this. How hard would it be for Pritchard to call London or send a fax that says, "Grade hard"? Not that they would make anything up, but they would look for every single possible defect they can detect. We have no control or appeal of the process. And you know, it only takes two bad reports for you to lose a third shipment. That could literally put somebody out of business. Now we don't know that this happens, but everybody knows that it could. They have that much power over us.

A Belizean grower described the relationship between the company and its allies more succinctly with a colorful Creole metaphor: "Fyffes and these men are the ass and the chamber pot. They are so stupid and selfish, they don't know when they've been shit on."

Growers who are unaffiliated with Fyffes widely acknowledge such fears of company retaliation; one of them even claimed that the scenario described by Seals has already come to pass. A BGA official observed, "Fyffes has already run two producers out of business, and a third is on the way out." Those two farmers were cut out of the fertilizer loan scheme and received a series of devastating quality scores after attempting to organize a growers' boycott of the company.[5] The third producer is Seals himself; he is a target because of his outspoken criticism of Fyffes in BGA meetings and during contract negotiations. While many growers feel that contracts with Fyffes's corporate competitors would improve their earnings, at least one BGA member is skeptical. Were a contract to be negotiated with anyone other than Fyffes, he predicted, its provisions might initially appear favorable, but it would eventually become little different from Fyffes's conditions. "When it comes right down to it," he observed with resignation, "the history of banana production in Central America here shows us one thing: all these multinationals treat growers in basically the same way, as servants."

CONCLUSIONS

Labor relations and working conditions on Central American banana farms have historically been among the harshest of any of the region's commercial agricultural sectors. As Bourgois (1989) observes, banana labor in the remote humid tropics is an unhealthy and dangerous undertaking because of environmental circumstances and the chemical-intensive nature of the industry. Yet Bourgois concludes, as did Kepner in the 1930s, that abuses of banana sector employment are attributable to the machinations and racism of United Fruit's North American managers. Predisposed to view nonwhite workers as less than fully human, plantation managers regard labor as merely another factor of production whose costs are to be minimized in the pursuit of sustained corporate profits.

This article has shown that neither the individual sentiments and identities of farm managers nor the structure of farm ownership have significant bearing on the conditions prevailing on Belizean banana farms, about 60 percent of which are owned by Belizeans themselves, with the remainder belonging to North American, Jamaican, or Danish investors of widely varying means and landholdings. While the industry's field workforce is overwhelmingly Hispanic Central American, about half of all farm managers are Belizeans and half are Central American immigrants. All but three of the country's twenty-three farms are independent of formal corporate management. Yet, despite the diversity of farming operations, all are governed by the imperative to minimize labor costs. On all farms, the necessity for cheap labor takes precedence over all other considerations; that imperative has resulted in the replication of the abusive forms of labor control documented on much larger plantations owned and managed by foreigners elsewhere in Central America.

The strategies of control and manipulation by which multinationals maintain supplies of fruit may appear remote from the farms on which the fruit itself is produced. Yet Fyffes's monopoly over the export of Belizean bananas allows it to dictate highly unfavorable terms of pricing and quality to Belizean growers. The local stratagems by which the banana multinational controls its "independent" suppliers in Belize and elsewhere are essential to its continued competitiveness and profitability in European markets. What emerges, then, from this description of the Belizean banana industry is a series of articulated, hierarchical relationships that extend from the boardrooms of multinational corporations to even the most remote banana farm in southern Belize.

The decisions and strategies taken at each level of this global-local articulation inevitably structure those below it. Having divided their regions of influence throughout Central America to ensure pricing monopolies, the banana multinationals nonetheless threaten incursions into each other's realms in order to benefit from current international marketing arrangements. In turn, each company zealously defends its control over private suppliers and seeks to deny them access to alternative buyers for their crops. In Belize, Fyffes maintains its local monopoly by cultivating strategic alliances with some growers and intimidating others into acquiescence. Finally, growers call upon similar strategies to lower labor costs through a well-considered combination of paternalism, paid informers, and outright intimidation. As seen here, corporate strategies that maintain local marketing monopolies pose grave threats to most farming operations, which survive on the thinnest of profit margins. Their survival, in turn, is gained at the cost of the economic well-being, as well as the health and human rights, of the workers who labor on them.

NOTES

This research was supported by a grant from the National Science Foundation (DBS-9211573), and was conducted in Belize between January and September 1993 and during a one-month return visit in 1995. I thank Ana Burgamy for her assistance in the field, as well as four residents of Cowpen (who must remain anonymous) for their help in conducting the household survey of farm workers. All individuals mentioned in this paper have been referred to by pseudonyms.

1. Bananas were first grown for export in Belize in the 1880s. Between 1911 and 1920, the United Fruit Company operated a 14,000-acre plantation in the

upper Stann Creek Valley (Moberg 1996a). This initial phase of banana production all but collapsed during the 1920s due to an outbreak of Panama disease.
2. The U.S.-based multinationals Chiquita, Dole, and Del Monte control 70
percent of the world banana trade (Trouillot 1988:159).
3. By law, Honduran banana workers must be paid a full month of additional
salary for each twelve months of work.
4. These preferences were challenged by the U.S. government and U.S.-
based banana multinationals in the World Trade Organization in 1995 and are
due to be phased out by 2002. Observers in Belize predict that the elimination
of the current EU preferences for ACP fruit will devastate the country's banana industry.
5. These growers were attempting to repeat the successful strategy of Belizean
citrus growers to obtain higher prices for their crops. Citrus producers in the
Stann Creek Valley staged a "growers' strike" in 1976 that forced the country's
processing companies to raise producer prices (Moberg 1990). Citrus growers
were able to play two competing processors against each other during the strike,
a strategy that would be impossible for banana growers facing Fyffes's monopoly power.

REFERENCES

Alonso, O. 1987. *Workers' Organization in the Banana Industry of Belize.* Belize
City: Society for Promotion of Education and Research.
Argueta, M. 1992. *La Historia de los sin Historia, 1900–1948.* Tegucigalpa:
Editorial Guaymuras.
Black, C., ed. 1984. *Jamaica's Banana Industry.* Kingston: Jamaica Banana
Producers' Association.
Bourgois, P. 1989. *Ethnicity at Work: Divided Labor on a Central American
Banana Plantation.* Baltimore: Johns Hopkins University Press.
Dosal, P. 1993. *Doing Business with Dictators: A Political History of United
Fruit in Guatemala, 1899–1944.* Wilmington, Del.: Scholarly Resources.
Echeverri-Gent, E. 1992. Forgotten Workers: British West Indians and the Early
Days of the Banana Industry in Costa Rica and Honduras. *Journal of Latin
American Studies* 24:275–308.
Grossman, L. 1998. *The Political Ecology of Bananas: Contract Farming, Peas-
ants, and Agrarian Change in the Eastern Caribbean.* Chapel Hill: Univer-
sity of North Carolina Press.
Holt, T. C. 1992. *The Problem of Freedom: Race, Labor, and Politics in Ja-
maica and Britain.* Baltimore: Johns Hopkins University Press.
Kepner, C. 1967 [1936]. *Social Aspects of the Banana Industry.* New York:
Columbia University Press.

Little, P. D. 1994. *Living under Contract: Contract Farming and Agrarian Transformation in Sub-Saharan Africa.* Madison: University of Wisconsin Press.

MacCameron, R. 1983. *Bananas, Labor, and Politics in Honduras, 1954–1963.* Syracuse, N.Y.: Maxwell School of Citizenship and Public Affairs, Syracuse University.

McCann, T. 1976. *An American Company: The Tragedy of United Fruit.* New York: Crown.

Moberg, M. 1990. Class Resistance and Class Hegemony: From Conflict to Co-optation in the Citrus Industry in Belize. *Ethnology* 29:189–208.

———. 1996a. Crown Colony as Banana Republic: The United Fruit Company in British Honduras, 1900–1920. *Journal of Latin American Studies* 28:357–81.

———. 1996b. Myths That Divide: Immigrant Labor and Class Segmentation in the Belizean Banana Industry. *American Ethnologist* 23:1–20.

———. 1996c. Transnational Labor Refugee Enclaves in a Central American Banana Industry. *Human Organization* 55:425–35.

———. 1997. *Myths of Ethnicity and Nation: Immigration, Work, and Identity in the Belize Banana Industry.* Knoxville: University of Tennessee Press.

Palacio, J. 1993. Social and Cultural Implications of Recent Demographic Changes in Belize. *Belizean Studies* 21:3–12.

Purcell, T. 1993. *Banana Fallout: Class, Color, and Culture among West Indians in Costa Rica.* Los Angeles: Center for Afro-American Studies, University of California at Los Angeles.

Trouillot, M-R. 1988. *Peasants and Capital: Dominica in the World Economy.* Baltimore: Johns Hopkins University Press.

Marshalltown, Iowa, and the Struggle for Community in a Global Age

Mark A. Grey

It is not unusual to observe processions of parishioners as they carry an image of the Virgin of Guadeloupe through the streets of some rural midwestern towns, although one would expect the participants to be Catholic and probably Hispanic. But in 1992, the procession following the Virgin in Marshalltown, Iowa, included a sizable number of Anglo Lutherans. Indeed, the procession was led by two members of the clergy in full vestments, one Lutheran and one Catholic. This march did not mark a mass conversion of some kind; it celebrated the transfer of the Virgin's statue from the basement of the Lutheran church to the Catholic church four blocks away. This ceremony climaxed nearly two years of ministry to a growing Latino community that was provided by a dedicated Lutheran pastor. When this pastor initially approached his Catholic counterpart about serving the newcomers, the priest's response was that Latinos could "come to mass in English" (Woodrick and Hartleip 1997). In order to meet the spiritual needs of Latinos, the Lutheran pastor started learning Spanish; in time he actually offered services in Spanish on Sunday afternoons. He even placed a statue of the Virgin in a corner of the church basement and built a small altar where people could pray, leave flowers, and light candles. Latinos called him Padre Juan. When he asked about limited participation in Holy Communion, Latinos told him they did not feel comfortable taking the host because there was no confessional, so he built one for them.

Alarmed at their pastor's accommodation of Latinos and their Catholic rituals, members of the congregation circulated a petition calling for his removal. He even received hate mail. One of his Anglo congregants even asked him when the Latinos were "going to become Christian" (Woodrick and Hartleip 1997). Finally realizing the need for a Latino ministry in Marshalltown, and probably tired of being upstaged by a

Lutheran, the Catholic Archdiocese installed a Spanish-speaking priest a few weeks before Padre Juan was due to leave. Between them, they worked out a transfer of both the ministry and the statue of the Virgin. Tired of the fighting, Padre Juan left his parish and the state. His remarkable story vividly illustrates the struggle for community in rural towns throughout the Midwest as they experience rapid influxes of minority immigrants and refugees. For the most part, the newcomers are responding to the hiring practices of meatpacking plants. Given the recent history of that industry, the arrival of the immigrants was inevitable. Virtually any community with a packing plant has become thoroughly integrated into a global labor market. But, as I will argue, social and institutional aspects of community have not kept up with this new economic reality.

Marshalltown is typical of these communities. It hosts a large pork packing operation that has hired hundreds of Latinos and other minorities since 1990, a policy that has presented numerous challenges to the institutions and social structure of the town. In order to appreciate Marshalltown's story, a brief introduction to contemporary packing towns is necessary.

MEATPACKING AND THE RURAL MIDWEST

Meatpacking jobs are characterized by low wages, difficult working conditions, high injury rates, and high turnover. When established residents refuse to take these jobs and unemployment rates are low, the plants seek others to hire. Latino immigrants, Southeast Asian refugees, and, more recently, African refugees are recruited. These workers are attractive to the industry for three essential reasons. First, packing jobs do not require English fluency, education, or previous job experience, so most immigrants are "qualified" to begin work as soon as they arrive. Second, immigrants who do not speak English constitute a segmented labor force because they have relatively few other opportunities in the job market and are forced to take low-wage positions. Third, immigrants and refugees are proficient at creating and maintaining the social networks necessary to ensure the economic viability of newcomers. In this way, the workforce can be supported in ways that do not cost the industry anything in extra wages. Among Southeast Asian refugees, these strategies typically involve extensive kin networks, while among Latinos the maintenance of home bases in Mexico and elaborate support networks along migratory routes are especially important (Grey 1996).

Some of the costs of maintaining the workforce are also passed on to the town. School districts are forced to create expensive new programs to accommodate increasing numbers of students who do not speak English. Low- to moderate-income housing often proves inadequate, forcing many newcomers to "double up," a situation that challenges local expectations of housing usage. Homeless shelters are established, along with other forms of social welfare, such as food banks (Gouveia and Stull 1995).

Rural packing towns also undergo dramatic social transitions as a result of high population transience and rapid diversification. High transience is primarily the result of employee turnover in the plants. A recent estimate for the entire red meat packing industry put annual turnover at 60 percent (Kay 1997), but this figure is probably too low. Such high turnover in the workforce is reflected in the constant movement of new and former workers and their families. When these people do not settle in the community, they do not have an opportunity to establish close ties with established residents. No common sense of "community" can emerge under such circumstances. Transience is also invoked as an explanation for rising rates of crime and domestic violence (Broadway 1990). Turnover can also have a profound impact on schools. Rapid student turnover disrupts instruction and complicates the allocation of resources and personnel.

Rapid diversification poses challenges as well. In Iowa, once predominantly Anglo and English-speaking towns now are more ethnically and linguistically varied. It is difficult to ascertain how many newcomers have arrived because most of the immigration has taken place since the 1990 census, and Census Bureau estimates are woefully inadequate. It might be possible to estimate the number by extrapolating from the size of the minority workforce in the plants, but most of the plants do not like to discuss such matters for public relations reasons. School enrollments are therefore the best source for data about the extent of immigration. Iowa has seven rural towns with large packing plants, and those school districts have collectively experienced a disproportionate amount of growth among students who do not speak English.

Between 1986 and 1996, the seven meatpacking towns experienced 343 percent growth in students who do not speak English (to a total of 6,654), accounting for 80.4 percent of the growth in such enrollments throughout the state. Growth in Spanish-speaking enrollments was even faster over the same period. The seven packing towns experienced 456 percent growth in this population, accounting for 64.4 percent of the growth in Spanish-speaking enrollments across the state. Even when urban districts are taken into account, these seven rural districts alone make up 30 percent of the state's rise in Spanish-speaking students.

MARSHALLTOWN, IOWA

Marshalltown hosts a large meatpacking plant, and it has experienced the same consequences as other rural packing towns. The local Swift and Company pork plant is the second largest in the state, providing more than 1,900 jobs, of which 1,650 are in production. Its 1996 payroll was nearly $49 million. The plant can slaughter up to 16,000 hogs per day and more than 3.6 million hogs in one year. In 1996 the plant produced 932.4 million pounds of pork products. In that same year, the plant's total sales were $787.8 million.

The plant started to hire Latinos in the early 1990s. The Latino workforce was initially small, but it now constitutes fully half of all production workers. The plant does not actively recruit in California, Texas, or Mexico as do some of the others, but it is still a magnet for migrant Latino workers. It also employs African Americans, Nuer refugees from Sudan, Southeast Asians, and Anglos. Estimates for the Latino population of Marshalltown range from 2,000 to 3,000, or between 8 and 12 percent of the town's 25,000 residents. In the 1990 census, there were fewer than 300. School enrollments reflect this growth as well, although enrollment growth seems to be coupled with high rates of student turnover. Enrollment analysis in Marshalltown's six elementary schools showed that two schools near the plant had only 33 percent of the district's students, but 54 percent of students had at least one parent who was employed at the meatpacking plant. Most important, these two schools had 48 percent of the students who transferred into or out of the district during the 1995–96 school year.

It is impossible to know how many people move through Marshalltown and how long they stay. In 1997, however, the annual turnover rate in the pork plant was 80 percent. It had previously been even higher, but the plant initiated a pay program that allowed new workers to earn the highest wages within about a month. Nevertheless, an 80 percent turnover rate means that the plant employs nearly 3,000 production workers even though there are only 1,650 production jobs in the plant.

Most of this turnover takes place in the first month on the job. Of all new hires in 1997, 33.5 percent quit within ninety days. Sixty-three percent of the latter quit within thirty days. On a typical day in 1998, 23 percent of production workers were employed less than one month, and a third of workers were employed less than ninety days. In all, two-thirds of the workforce was employed less than one year. When workers turn over at such rapid rates, it is no wonder that hundreds of them never put down roots. The result is that most never develop a sense of Marshalltown as "home."

High turnover rates raise a question about whether newcomers want to settle in town. An analysis of plant data between October 1996 and September 1997 indicated that turnover is high among all ethnic groups in the plant. Indeed, 41 percent of all workers who quit simply abandon their jobs. They do not show up for work, they do not return from a leave of absence, or they walk off the line. There are, however, some differences between Anglo and Latino quitting behaviors. The median tenure of Latinos (seventy days) is twice as high as that of Anglos. In addition, only 23 percent of Latinos quit or are fired within thirty days, although 44 percent of Anglos fit this category.

Articulating the differences between Latino and Anglo quitting patterns is important in helping us understand the nature of relations between Latinos and established residents. Most Anglos in the Swift plant have little education and few job skills; as such, they are relatively unattractive on the job market. Even in a climate of low unemployment, many of these workers take packinghouse jobs as a last resort. Moreover, a high percentage (70 percent) of Anglos who quit are unmarried, suggesting that they work only long enough to earn some money and then drift to some other job. Indeed, higher wages seemed to encourage Anglos to apply and then stick with the job; on the other hand, no long-term pattern of employment emerged. Yet there was a popular stereotype that Anglos at least had some incentive to stay on the job because they had familial and other obligations in the area.

Another part of this stereotype is that Latinos lack these local ties, which is why they can quit so often. Many Anglos in the plant expressed bitterness about this perceived lack of commitment; they said that Latinos would make packing jobs "seasonal" if they could. What this Anglo stereotype did not take into account was that most Latinos had the same kinds of obligations as Anglos, but these ties were not necessarily in Marshalltown. Packing jobs have attracted Latinos because they are easy to obtain, the wages are high relative to those in Mexico, and rural Iowa is safe and has good schools. Yet despite these attractions, most Latinos quit often and leave the area. What Anglos in the plant did not appreciate was that quitting is an integral part of Latino migration strategies. Instead of being irresponsible, most Latinos quit because they have responsibilities elsewhere. This migratory strategy allows Latinos to use the plant to accumulate some wealth and still maintain home bases where that wealth can be used to greater effect.

Given a propensity to migrate, Latinos are also able to take advantage of several plants in the region. As long as plants need their labor, Latinos can safely quit one job, take time off to migrate, and then find work at another plant at roughly the same wage. In many cases, workers return to the same plant with the reasonable assurance that they will be rehired. One Anglo manager described this expectation as "irrational," but quitting and returning to the same plant some weeks or months later is a perfectly rational part of Latino migration. Anglo managers in the plant do not fully understand that when workers go home to Mexico, they pass on information about jobs and support networks along the way. Migrating Latinos become de facto recruiters for the plant as they establish a pipeline of workers. The plant clearly benefits from this connection, since a full third of production workers are from the same town, Villa Chuato in the state of Michoacan.

There is evidence that some Latino families are settling in Marshalltown. Banks employ Spanish translators to provide mortgages, for example, and in 1997 approximately twenty-five houses were sold to Latino families. There are also several Latino entrepreneurs operating grocery stores, restaurants, auto repair shops, a bar, and a western wear shop. Most Latinos, however, seem not to be staying in the town for extended periods; many continue to migrate between Mexico and Marshalltown.

This migratory link has forged an unofficial sister-city relationship between Villa Chuato and Marshalltown, a link most Anglos seem to know nothing about. Unlike formal sister cities, Marshalltown and Villa Chuato do not exchange gifts or visits by official delegations. Instead, their relationship is based on mutual economic need: the plant needs Latino workers and the workers need the plant. Marshalltown happens to be the town that links them. The Marshalltown economy has long relied on international markets for its manufactures, but the influx of Latinos marks the town's integration into a global labor market as well. Out of necessity, the pork plant is still in the process of coming to terms with this reality. In order to ensure the viability of the town's largest employer, Marshalltown will also have to adjust to Latinos and make them a part of the community.

ACCOMMODATING LATINOS
AND PROMOTING ACCORD

As the story of Padre Juan demonstrates, the influx of Latinos challenges the community. Some residents and community leaders have responded by trying to promote accommodation of and accord with the newcomers. Since the mid-1990s in particular, a relative handful of private citizens, officials, and businesses have led the way. What follows is a brief history of their trials and tribulations.

In 1996 the Marshalltown newspaper started publishing a Spanish-language edition, *La Voz de Comunidad.* This paper filled three important needs: it provided a source of news about Mexico and the world with AP and other wire service stories; it provided useful information about local services and programs; and it gave businesses an opportunity to advertise in the growing Latino market. Most ads were bought by used car dealers, banks, and grocery stores. The Swift plant also placed job announcements. But after only seven months, the paper was canceled. It never generated a profit, and it was shut down when it lost a total of $10,000. The publisher told a group of concerned citizens that the paper could not sell enough advertising to be viable. He blamed this failure on the biased attitudes of many local business owners.

Another important development in 1996 was the formation of an active diversity committee that included representatives from the city, county, school district, Chamber of Commerce, and community college. They were joined by a smaller group, the Hispanic Task Force, which had formed at the Catholic church. Together they formed the Marshalltown Diversity Committee (MDC), which chose a mission statement: "To strengthen the community of Marshalltown by recognizing and embracing diversity." In many respects, the MDC was like similar committees in other meatpacking towns that had formed in the wake of rapid diversification. The organization of the MDC was timely. Just two months after the group was formed, the Immigration and Naturalization Service (INS) raided the Swift plant. It was the largest INS raid in Iowa's history, and 148 workers, both male and female, were arrested. Plant management fully cooperated with the INS and identified 300 illegal immigrants on the workforce. In order to facilitate the raid, the plant even made arrangements to call in suspected employees to work on Saturday afternoon. After they were gathered in the cafeteria, detainees were taken for processing to a National Guard armory in another town. The raid caused a great deal of stress and confusion among Latinos. Families were divided. Some spouses were unable to see each other before one or the other was deported. Children found themselves stranded without either parent. Even Latinos who were in the country legally feared deportation. The raid generated a good deal of controversy in Marshalltown and around the state.

In response to this situation, the MDC pulled together Latinos, Anglos, police officers, civic and business leaders, union leaders, service providers, and researchers to discuss the raid and its aftermath. The committee provided an open forum to air different perspectives on the event. Latinos were given a chance to express their frustration and anger to local officials, including the police, who cooperated with the raid. Anglo citizens and city officials tried to assure Latinos that they were still welcome. Information was exchanged and everyone involved was able to develop a clearer sense of what had happened.

However therapeutic this session might have been, it left many questions unanswered. Despite the very best intentions of local officials and citizens, the raid was a product of federal policy and had been instigated by the INS and the U.S. attorney's office. In order to bring their perspectives into the mix, the MDC arranged for an additional open forum with the director of the regional INS office in Omaha. The meeting was well attended, with more than 100 people present. A number of Latinos came, as did some city officials and union leaders. After some introductory remarks, the INS official gave some background to the raid. He was very careful to explain the plant's cooperation and how the civil rights of detainees were ensured by the presence of members of the Iowa Commission on Latino Civil Rights. Subsequent discussion centered around immigration policy. Some anger was expressed by both Anglos and Latinos, and the union accused the INS of discrimination because Anglo workers had been passed through the check point on the basis of skin color alone. Union leaders were also angry that they were not allowed access to their members who were in detention. But, as the INS official made clear, the INS was under no legal obligation to allow such contact.

The raid and its aftermath further complicated Latino-Anglo relations.

The INS forum proved successful in that it cleared up matters of policy and procedure, but it also left a very clear message: Latinos in the country illegally do not deserve the same treatment as those who are documented. Even supporters of diversity initiatives recognized that illegal immigrants were unlikely to see the benefits of those initiatives. As long as civil rights were ensured, many in Marshalltown (both Anglo and Latino) were willing to make distinctions between deserving and undeserving immigrants. This attitude clashed with the point of view of most Latinos and some service providers, to whom such distinctions were fundamentally irrelevant. To them, the INS raid made it clear that the central question was not legal but concerned human rights. As a poster in one Latino restaurant read, "No Human Being Is Illegal."

The INS raid drove home the fact that the border between Mexico and the United States formed an arbitrary political barrier, but it meant nothing in terms of economic interdependence. Indeed, the INS actions, which raised the specter of illegal immigration, did little but feed negative stereotypes and suspicions about Latinos. INS raids across the state revealed how deeply dependent packing plants are on Latino immigrants. Most criticism in the state and local press, however, targeted the immigrants and not the plants. Only a few academics (such as myself) and some outspoken citizens questioned this apparent hypocrisy. Very few openly acknowledged that meatpacking could not survive without immigrants, even though immigrants in general took the political heat when so many were discovered to be in the country illegally. Most critics sought deportation for the illegal migrants. Very few believed settlement of immigrants was the answer.

Nonetheless, some Marshalltown citizens initiated efforts to legalize immigrants. St. Mary's Catholic Church started a Hispanic Ministries office to meet the day-to-day needs of Latinos and to facilitate their applications for green cards and citizenship. This office is operated by a priest and a nun, both Spanish speakers, on a shoestring budget. They received training in INS procedures and maintain a full supply of INS and State Department application materials. They also bought fingerprinting equipment and became certified by the federal government to take prints for applicants' files.

The community college has been active as well. For example, it offers English as a Second Language (ESL) classes. For a while, these classes were offered at the plant. The college also sponsored a "Dance of Diversity Conference" in 1996; its purpose was to inform participants about Latino culture, demographic change, and related issues such as health and education. Such diversity conferences are well intentioned, but usually superficial. For the most part, discussion of "culture" is anecdotal. The conferences also tend to reach those people who are already working with immigrants; the sessions amount to preaching to the choir. Valuable information is certainly shared, but such activities do not generally influence ordinary citizens. Moreover, they avoid the most difficult questions about economic integration, class, and racism, unless extreme views are shared by self-appointed spokesmen for minority groups. Such discourse, however, is often counterproductive, as rural Iowans do not like to be considered racist just because they are white or have little interaction with Latinos.

The conference was held shortly after a particularly difficult chapter in the history of Latino Marshalltown. Low-income housing in the town has been difficult to find for several years. A small trailer court on the south side of town attracted many Latinos because of low rents. The trailers were old and in bad shape. The owner of the land upon which the court was situated—an older Anglo woman—decided to eliminate the trailers and turn the land over to the city for park space. Although the court had been in operation for decades, the owner decided to have it torn down. Sensing that her decision was based on racist bias, members of the Latino community protested at public hearings. There were a number of sympathetic responses, but the city was powerless to block the owner's decision, and the families who lived in the trailers were forced to find housing elsewhere.

Stereotypes about Latinos set up other barriers. Crime rates, for example, rose during the 1990s, and there is a perception that the Latino influx has been to blame. Such stereotypes are fed by the press and law enforcement officials. Indeed, the police chief was often quoted in the local media to the effect that the prevalence of illegal migrants was linked to the rise in methamphetamine distribution. His source of information was the Federal Drug Enforcement Agency and not local statistics. A Swift plant manager aptly referred to these statements as "xenophobic saber rattling." Since stereotypes about Latinos rarely distinguish between "illegals" and others, the message was that crime rates were up and drug use was rampant because of Latinos. When the police chief appeared before the MDC, however, he admitted that his department's computer database does not even allow for tracking ethnicity or race, so there could be no statistical evidence to support the contention that Latinos commit a disproportionate amount of crime.

This small victory against the stereotypes was overshadowed less than a week later when drugs and Marshalltown were featured in the news magazine *U.S. News and World Report* (McGraw 1998) and in the *Des Moines Register* (Zeleny 1998). Both stories exposed the transportation of methamphetamines from Mexico to Marshalltown via California. Marshalltown had become a major distribution center for the Midwest. The *U.S. News and World Report* piece in particular played on the contrast between the ideal small town and the new drug trade. The author implied that the Mexicans, fearing that sooner or later they will be deported anyway, decide to make quick cash by "selling meth to the crazy gringo tweakers." He claimed that although a few of the Mexicans were outright agents of Mexican drug gangs, most of those who ended up dealing drugs had simply fallen into the job because "it is easier to sell meth than to cut up hogs for $7 an hour" (McGraw 1998:34).

Members of the MDC disagreed about whether this coverage was a setback for ethnic relations. Most concluded that it fed stereotypes among those who had already made up their minds. Others pointed out that Marshalltown had had a drug problem for years and that local law enforcement and the press were picking up the story now because of Latino involvement. The mayor, an active member of the MDC, expressed outrage at the source of the reporters' information: a county sheriff whose jurisdiction did not even include Marshalltown.

One other potential setback concerned open enrollment of Anglo students out of the Marshalltown school district. School board members were concerned that this practice was a form of "white flight" resulting from the growth in immigrant enrollments. A formal survey of families who took their children out of the district demonstrated, however, that parents rarely did so because of concerns about minorities. Indeed, the vast majority simply moved their children to smaller districts or to schools closer to their rural residences (Grey 1997). The local press covered the open enrollment issue and generally blamed it on the violence in the schools, which was also subtly linked to Latino enrollments. One commentator noted, "Some parents are doing more than transferring their kids to outlying districts: one Marshalltown family sold their home on the northwest side and built a new house in [a town twenty miles away] this year after one of their daughters was assaulted by an illegal immigrant while playing at Rogers School" (Graham 1997:33–34).

THE HARD PART IS YET TO COME

Despite these setbacks, those dedicated to diversity press on. The Baptist church started a Latino ministry, complete with Spanish-language services and ESL instruction. The MDC applied for and received funding from Ecumenical Ministries of Iowa to support ESL classes, legalization efforts, and revolving loans for newcomers to pay housing deposits.

Members of the MDC noticed that despite their many efforts to include Latinos, including providing translation services, Latin attendance at their meetings dropped off. They came to realize that any meaningful outreach would have to take place on a personal basis. Praiseworthy dedication and willingness to develop relations with newcomers cannot always overcome differences in language, culture, residential status, and class. Personal relationships between established residents and Latinos are being formed at work, in the neighborhoods, in churches, and in the schools. Indeed, one elementary school prides itself on the prevalence of bilingual birthday parties. But it is difficult to predict how long it will take for these relationships to develop more widely.

It may take a generation. But as long as most Latinos do not settle in Marshalltown and continue to rely on return migration to Mexico, it will be difficult for them to develop a sense of community in the town. This point seems lost on many Anglos, who view the immigrant experience in terms of their own family histories. Their European ancestors came to rural Iowa, settled, raised families, and formed lasting communities. Similar arguments are made about learning English: "My grandparents had to learn English, so why can't the Mexicans?" But the more recent arrivals come under different economic and legal circumstances. For European immigrants earlier in this century, Iowa was a destination. For most Latinos, Marshalltown is not an end point but only one part of a migration strategy that does not involve permanent resettlement. Indeed, Latinos have few incentives to settle in Marshalltown because the cost of living is high and their wages do not go as far as they might in Mexico. What seems to escape most Anglos is the fact that Marshalltown is only one piece of the pattern; it is not the entire picture, as it had been for previous generations.

THE FUTURE

There is no reason to think that the pork packing plant will stop needing immigrant workers. The more critical question is whether Latinos will actually settle in town and not simply work there from time to time. This consideration seems to be an important factor in stabilizing the plant's workforce. Latino families are settling in each year, although the evidence suggests that most of them maintain close ties with their sending communities in Mexico. It is not yet clear whether these families will one day come to consider Marshalltown "home."

Such an outcome will depend in no small part on the availability of low-cost houses for purchase. Marshalltown has a chronic housing shortage at all income levels, although there are no proposals to build new low-income housing units and there is a countywide moratorium on new mobile home courts. Elderly Anglos occupy most low- to moderate-income housing, and many of them could move up to higher cost housing if it becomes available. But such a shift depends on the development of new units so that established residents can move out of housing that Latinos (and other packers) can afford. The lack of affordable housing has already spread the Swift workforce beyond Marshalltown. In January 1998, production workers lived in 100 different zip codes.

Another important part of Latino settlement involves religion. Some of these efforts have already been discussed. Some Latinos, particularly those with evangelical or charismatic inclinations, are forming their own churches. Indeed, there is already a Spanish-speaking Pentecostal church located in a downtown storefront. Changes in law enforcement will also be necessary. In 1998 the police department hired its first Spanish-speaking patrol officer, who is expected to facilitate positive relations with law-abiding Latinos and to help diminish some of the stereotyped connections between the newcomers and crime. Marshalltown schools are already creating programs for newcomers, including ESL classes and special after-school activities. As recent enrollment trends in Marshalltown and other packing towns suggest, the percentage of minority newcomers will probably continue to rise, necessitating more accommodations for their children in the schools.

Marshalltown's integration into the global labor market seems irreversible. Even with the efforts by the MDC, city leaders, churches, and other concerned citizens, the social integration of Marshalltown's Latino population will probably not be complete for at least another generation or two. The result is that at least in the near future, there will be two Marshalltowns, one Anglo and the other Latino.

REFERENCES

Broadway, M. 1990. Meatpacking and Its Consequences for Garden City, Kansas, in the 1980s. *Urban Anthropology* 19(4):321–44.

Gouveia, L., and D. D. Stull. 1995. Dances with Cows: Beefpacking's Impact on Garden City, Kansas, and Lexington, Nebraska. In *Any Way You Cut It: Meat Processing and Small-Town America,* ed. D. Stull, M. Broadway, and D. Griffith, pp. 85–107. Lawrence: University of Kansas Press.

Graham, L. J. 1997. Letter from Lynda: Open Enrollment—Why Are There More "Out" than "In"? *Marshalltimes,* December:33–34.

Grey, M.A. 1996. Patronage, Kinship, and Recruitment in the Migration of Lao and Mennonite Labor to Storm Lake, Iowa. *Culture and Agriculture* 18(1):14–18.

————. 1997. *Open Enrollment Survey.* Marshalltown, Iowa: Marshalltown Community Schools.

Kay, S. 1997. The Nature of Turnover: Packers Attempt to Reverse a Financial Drain. *Meat and Poultry,* September: 30–34.

McGraw, D. 1998. The Iowa Connection: Powerful Mexican Drug Cartels Have Hit Rural America. *U.S. News and World Report* 124:33–36.

Woodrick, A. C., and J. E. Hartleip. 1997. *Constructing Religious Communities: A Preliminary Explanation of Hispanic Ministry in Iowa.* Paper presented at the annual meeting of the Religious Research Association, San Diego.

Zeleny, J. 1998. Drug Takes the Long Road: Meth Funneled via I-80 Pipeline. *Des Moines Register,* February 27:1A, 4A.

Deindustrialization, Job Displacement, and Contested Ideology of Work in a Southern Town

Tara Skipper

In times of crisis, people frequently articulate values and beliefs about their lives that are otherwise not addressed. In Maycomb, Alabama,[1] the community as a whole and the working class in particular have been experiencing a crisis that has prompted questions about the way in which the value of work is understood. It has also led people to reconsider the responsibilities that link the community and a major corporation. Maycomb's workers have been displaced from apparel manufacturing jobs, and they dispute the ways in which the company management and local elites have conceptualized the value of their work. The literature on deindustrialization and job displacement suggests that this contested ideology is unusual, although that ideology, in addition to resources and motivation, may allow displaced workers in Maycomb to respond collectively to the crisis in the near future.

COMPANY AND COMMUNITY: HISTORY OF A RELATIONSHIP

Maycomb (pop. 7,014) has been home to Glenwood Mills, manufacturers of women's intimate apparel, since 1938 when the company sought to escape a unionizing labor force in the Northeast and to secure cheap labor in the South. The sewing plant was the company's first installation in Maycomb, which eventually became the partial corporate headquarters for Glenwood Mills in 1969. It provided rural white women with their first industrial employment opportunities and "got them out of the cotton fields," as a state politician was fond of saying. Income from women's work in sewing allowed farm families to brick in their houses and later purchase automobiles and refrigerators. The new jobs were credited by the county farm extension agent with saving the family farms themselves.

Glenwood Mills integrated its workforce in 1965, and for the first time black women in Maycomb County had the option of remaining in their home community while working at a job that paid more, entailed more prestige, and was easier than work as a domestic or as a fieldhand. Women's income in the black community allowed families to buy automobiles, improve their houses, and participate in American consumer culture. The composition of the sewing plant workforce had risen to approximately 70 percent African American by 1995.

Community leaders in Maycomb welcomed Glenwood Mills with open arms in 1938 and provided incentives for the company to locate there. The Alabama State Planning Commission was created in 1935 to subsidize industry, and the town itself raised money through bonds to build a plant that would be leased and eventually bought by the company. Local ownership of the plant and the company policy of recruiting labor exclusively through community leaders (first among whites, and then in both white and black communities) reinforced the local class hierarchy, thereby creating a situation in which trade unionization of the rank-and-file workforce could never take hold.

Maycomb was proud to be a "company town," and incentives for Glenwood Mills have continued throughout the years. The company has received abatements and tax breaks through the Industrial Development and the Wallace-Kater Acts. The county has granted numerous property tax breaks over the years, and the city has sunk new wells and installed a new water treatment plant specifically for the Glenwood Mills dyehouse.

Other advantages have been "under the table." The local weekly newspaper, the *Maycomb Journal,* has always charged Glenwood Mills at three times the regular cost of advertising; in return, the company is guaranteed perpetually favorable coverage and extensive reporting of any of its "good works" in the community. Moreover, certain community leaders may have actively kept out industries that could have competed for labor with Glenwood Mills.

Management announced the closing of the Maycomb sewing plant in 1995 following shutdowns in four other small towns in southern Alabama. When the plant was finally closed in 1997, 660 women were put out of work. Like other apparel manufacturers, Glenwood Mills has played its part in a changing world capitalist system by relocating its sewing plants to Mexico, Guatemala, and Honduras. In these new Third World plants, women sew without air conditioning, receive no benefits, and earn seventy cents per hour, compared with seven dollars per hour in Alabama.

Given its history as a company town, Maycomb went into a state of shock at this announcement. Community leaders were angry with Glenwood Mills' management, which had not consulted with them about its plans. Nonetheless, community leaders and the upper class soon actively promoted the ideology set out by Glenwood Mills' management about the move of the sewing plant and its relationship and responsibility to the community.

CONTESTED IDEOLOGY OF WORK: GLENWOOD MILLS' MANAGEMENT AND COMMUNITY LEADERS

The viewpoint promoted by Glenwood Mills' management and community leaders is one that draws on American ideology about the nature and value of the capitalist system and industrial development. The president of the company[2] praised the "work ethic" in Maycomb, and said that he would like to have held on to sewing jobs in the town, but could not do so "out of survival." He pointed out that Glenwood Mills' competition has been manufacturing in the Third World for ten years and that it was necessary to do likewise in order to compete. Nonetheless, he asserted that the company's management was "not a cold-blooded group of MBAs" but rather local people who had worked with the company throughout their lives. They did not want to make these tough decisions, but saw no other choice.

The president claimed to be responsible to the "person on the street," presumably a potential customer, and to the stockholder—not to the workers. The company has taken the position that, because the workers identify with the products they make, and therefore with the company, they should be happy that the company is financially healthy. This ideology is based on the assumption of capitalist culture and formal economic theory that capitalism is not only profitable but inherently *good*. According to a college-level textbook in managerial economics, "Firms exist by public consent to serve the needs of society. Only through the satisfactory execution of this mandate will business survive and prosper" (Pappas and Hirschey 1990:13). The decision to relocate the sewing plant is one that must be good because the company is prospering as a result. Furthermore, "firms and individuals whose objective is to do well (earn profits) end up doing good (causing economic betterment) in the process. Far from being abhorrent, enlightened self-interest is the means by which all benefit" (Pappas and Hirschey 1990:15).

An important official on the Maycomb County Industrial Development Board promoted another perspective on this identification of worker welfare with company financial health. He said, "This is a good time for people to go out and buy [our] brand. We all need to support the company." He is continuing the trend of promoting worker and community identification with the company even if the latter is no longer promoting its identification with Maycomb County workers. He also chose to draw on the frequently documented feelings of displaced workers that they are to blame for their situation (Newman 1988; Nash 1989; Pappas 1989). He said, "What has happened is a good example of what can happen when we don't support Alabama companies." The responsibility for the move is ideologically shifted to the workers as consumers rather than as laborers, and the company is absolved of responsibility.

The ideology is based on the view that Maycomb is identified with Glenwood Mills and that the management has the town's best interests at heart. As a result, it has been argued that the closing of the sewing plant may mean not only the preservation of the company itself but ultimately the preservation of jobs for Maycomb. According to a company official, "Shutting this plant down will save some jobs in the long run." The argument that Glenwood Mills is acting to protect the jobs (in dyeing, cutting, and distribution) that remain in Maycomb has a gendered dimension because they are men's jobs, whereas sewing jobs are exclusively held by women. The implication is that women should be willing to sacrifice their jobs in order to preserve the jobs of their husbands, sons, and other male relatives. The president advanced a similar argument by saying, "Some [households] may determine that the extra income wasn't totally necessary." In this way, management utilizes capitalist ideology that defines women's work as "supplemental," thereby not essential, and justifies lower wages and expendability (Hartmann 1981).

CONTESTED IDEOLOGY OF WORK: THE UPPER CLASS

Many upper-class people in Maycomb feel sorry for those who have lost jobs; they believe that Glenwood Mills has not acted in good faith. Nevertheless, they have ultimately accepted and elaborated on management's interpretation of the situation. They choose to emphasize the company's past contributions—"it was a lifesaver for this community"—rather than any current obligations. The upper class must accept management's interpretation of the situation, not only because of the "corporate hegemony" (Nash 1989) of Glenwood Mills in the town but also because of their own position in the class and racial hierarchy. Glenwood Mills' managers are peers of the upper class. Most upper-class people view managers as individuals, saying, "The new friends that came to run the company were such decent, really first-class people." They do not know workers personally and consider them socially inferior. As a result, the upper class can feel sorry for those losing jobs, but they cannot completely sympathize, for doing so would destroy the ideological justification of their social position. Upper-class people are supposed to have "worked their way up," while those in the working class are "lazy."

In Maycomb, there is also a racial component to the emphasis on Glenwood Mills' past contributions to community development. The white elite emphasizes what the company did for past workers because those workers were white. As such, they were not only more deserving and hardworking but also more likely to move up in the local class hierarchy. For example, people in the upper class frequently point out that the mother of a prominent local politician worked as a sewing machine operator for forty years to support her children, and "look where he is as a result."

The ideology that capitalism is inherently a social "good" also appeals to class status, since it is associated with the view on the nature of capitalism provided by a college education in business or economics. As a result, any competing ideology is automatically disvalued as an incomplete and ignorant understanding of the situation. The idea is that "you can't take it personally" if you lose your job; doing so demonstrates that one is hopelessly lacking the knowledge that competition in the market system is inherently good for everyone.

CONTESTED IDEOLOGY OF WORK:
SEWING MACHINE OPERATORS

Most displaced sewing operators are not influenced by the "educated view." When the mayor was quoted as saying, "This is not the first place that has been closed," one former worker said, "When she said that, I could have stuck my foot up her tootie, because that's not right for her to say that. She's got a job, she's got money, we don't have nothing, and I'd like for her to have my job."

Before the announcement that the plant would close, sewing machine operators remained hopeful that Glenwood Mills would retain the Maycomb plant, despite the closing of neighboring operations. Since Maycomb was a company town, workers thought that their plant would be the last of the company's operations in the South to be moved to the Third World. Workers described the pain of losing jobs they had counted on to support their families. In one woman's words, "It wasn't a shock to me, but it was kind of a sense of loss. You put thirty-one years on the job, and all of a sudden you are no longer there, and you're fifty-one years old. What do you do? You can't retire, and who is going to hire you at that age?" She added, "In my heart, all the way down to my toes, it was a sad feeling, you know. You've been there that long, and then all of a sudden they come and tell you you don't have a future, a job, and that's all you've been depending on all these years."

Women felt that the company was accountable to the people who were responsible for its success: the workers who made the products. This identification with the products and the company had been actively fostered by Glenwood Mills throughout its years in Maycomb, and no doubt was partially responsible for a lack of union activity. Indeed, sewing operators *have* taken pride in the merchandise they have manufactured. They described working long hours and even overtime, putting their "heart and soul" into their work.

As a result of this pride, sewing operators argue that the company had a responsibility to them, yet "throwed them to the dogs." Nonetheless, workers are savvy enough about the nature of the capitalist system to know why they are losing their jobs: in Mexico, Glenwood Mills can pay workers one-tenth of their wages and provide no benefits whatsoever. Moreover, workers understand the reality of the historical relationship between Glenwood Mills and the Maycomb upper class. One younger woman worker said, "This is a slap in our face. It really hurts because other businesses that would have brought jobs to the county have been kept out to protect Glenwood Mills. Now they're taking our jobs to Mexico."

They blame the company for ignoring their hard work and the relationship it represented. Nevertheless, they understand that, despite their efforts, Glenwood Mills has no incentive to remain. Rather, displaced sewing operators for the most part blame the government. According to one woman, "After NAFTA first hit, somebody from Mobile came through the mill interviewing, and I said, 'I don't think we should give up our jobs. That's what this is all about—they're going to take our jobs.' 'No, they're not going to do that,' but you see that's what happened, they got our jobs."

Another woman said,

> For my opinion, I feel that it was unfair, that we got a raw deal because they are taking everything to Mexico for cheaper labor and actually I just feel like the United States shouldn't allow places like Mexico to come in and take our jobs because the companies want to make more money. They aren't concerned about the people. We have to live here. And they are moving our jobs and taking them to Mexico for nothing and then send them back here and we are the people ending up having to buy the goods.

The sewing plant remained open an additional year after it was scheduled to close because of the need to turn out a particularly popular and fashionable item. As a result, workers were laid off slowly, without regard to their seniority at the plant. The company asserted that retaining one's job or being transferred to another division with Glenwood Mills would be contingent on merit alone, but the sewing operators felt that this practice was unfair. A young woman said, "I guess they figured that they'll get retirement in a couple of years, they don't need to work, but I think the young ones, like myself, should have been gone first. I think the people that only had two or three years left, I think they should have been the ones, because they are the ones that had been there for over twenty or thirty years."

IDEOLOGY OF WORK, COMPARATIVE CASES OF JOB DISPLACEMENT, AND COLLECTIVE ACTION

What does it mean that apparel workers and management (and its upper-class allies) hold different ideologies about the nature, meaning, and value of work? The workers identify with their products, yet contest management's definitions of their work and its value. The move of the sewing plant to the Third World has demonstrated to them their position in the world capitalist system. Their craftsmanship does not create the special relationship with the company that they might have liked. These women understand what is happening to them. They are aware of their exploitation. This awareness, however, is still individual rather than collective.

Comparison with other cases of job displacement as a result of deindustrialization demonstrates that such awareness is unusual. Displaced workers in Maycomb blame the company and the government, while in other case studies, the laid-off workers blame themselves (Pappas 1989; Newman 1988; Nash 1989). For example, Newman describes a situation in which workers were displaced when the Singer sewing machine plant closed in Elizabeth, New Jersey. They blamed their own abandonment of quality in craftsmanship, in favor of quantity of production, for the decline of the company. Singer workers understood the decline of the company as a morality lesson about what happens to a company, a community, and a country when traditional values are ignored. According to workers, management was no longer drawn from the ranks and therefore had no commitment to workers. The new management "forgot that it was the craftsmanship of the Elizabeth employees that gave Singer its preeminent position in the sewing machine market" (Newman 1988:185). Nash interviewed General Electric employees in Pittsfield, Massachusetts, when their plant closed after a century. They did not blame the company, but criticized themselves. They felt that the company had a responsibility only to make money, not to benefit workers.

Both Nash and Newman describe communities in the urban Northeast where blue-collar jobs have led to middle-class affluence. The displaced workers in their studies were almost exclusively white men, and the jobs from which they were laid off were unionized. Yet these "heroic male factory workers" (di Leonardo 1985:237) appear to be more accepting of management and elite ideology about the nature of the capitalist system and their part in it than are displaced sewing machine operators in Maycomb. Perhaps as men defined as the breadwinners in their households, these displaced workers felt that they had failed to live up to their gender role. Working-class men may be unlikely to see themselves as exploited victims of the capitalist system or of company management. Therefore, *they* must be responsible for the job loss and their failure as men. If the American work world is indeed a meritocracy, and if they had lived up to the American dream by working hard, then they must have lost their jobs because they could no longer compete. Due to their working/middle-class position, these men are also more likely to subscribe to the "educated view" that capitalism is inherently good and that companies have a right to concern themselves only with profit. The combination of these two ideologies could have resulted in the feeling that they could not compete as a labor force and cannot compete as men in American society.

This ideology is unlikely to lead to collective action against the company or the system. Comparing American workers affected by deindustrialization with the working class in the Third World, Nash (1994:23) concludes:

> Pittsfield workers are among the least conscious of their condition in the global system and the most subject to hegemonic control that vitiates their actions in defense of their interests. With the decline of the General Electric plant in their area, they retreat into *privatized misery* rather than, as the miners of Bolivia, protesting publicly the lack of responsibility of the mining corporation [emphasis added].

The "privatized misery" experienced by displaced male workers in the cases described above is unlikely to result in collective social action due to structural barriers created by institutions previously designed to defend their interests—unions. In the United States, unions traded their right to participate in decisions (such as a plant closing) that affect the entire company for the right to negotiate shop floor issues, such as wages and hours. In heavy industries, this social contract resulted in high union wages and generous benefits, but left workers without a voice in the way their work is organized. As a result, the closing of unionized plants leaves unions with their role restricted to the negotiation of benefits for displaced workers rather than to the protest against the decision itself. In the case of the steel industry, Camp (1995:16) asserts that "unions actually discouraged steel workers from taking direct action in response to steel mill closings." Moreover, in some cases where workers did initiate direct action, unions worked against them (Hathaway 1993).

Displaced women workers in Maycomb are experiencing the "privatized misery" described by Nash, but compared with the men in her study, they are less subject to personal feelings of responsibility and guilt in not fulfilling the American dream and not fulfilling their gender role. This "misery," without feelings of inadequacy, may provide a situation in which they can draw upon the resources that are available to them to improve the conditions of their lives in the near future.

Ginsburg (1989:39) has suggested that personal "life crises," resulting from socioeconomic change, may prompt self-reflection:

Life reviews . . . may be compelling during critical shifts that occur throughout the life course, particularly when there is a dissonance between such moments and cultural definitions for them. These "life crises"—"transitions from one culturally defined stage of life to another at which there is regularly experienced individual stress" (Silverman 1975:309)—may reveal contention over cultural definitions. This sense of life crisis may be even more likely in situations of rapid change when the social rules for an assumed life trajectory are called into question.

Ginsburg finds, in the "procreation stories" of pro- and anti-abortion activists in Fargo, North Dakota, that these "life crises" were often points of departure for political activism. In Maycomb, cultural definitions of the nature of corporate responsibility and product value are clearly in flux. Moreover, the move of Glenwood Mills is resulting in local socioeconomic change. Former sewing machine operators *do* "take it personally" and, as a result, are questioning and refashioning the trajectory of their lives. They expected to work for Glenwood Mills until their retirement, but now they must redirect their plans. Ginsburg's example serves to demonstrate how an internalization of socioeconomic crisis may, in the end, result in political activism. Individual consciousness of exploitation might be enough to drive these women to action.

The cross-cultural literature, however, demonstrates that "exploited classes . . . are not inherently revolutionary, nor reformist . . . or anything. What they become is a function of the institutions and values available to them" (Worsley 1984:232). The women workers at Glenwood Mills would not seem to have institutions available to them that might serve as means through which to protest their situation; research, however, suggests that institutions and networks that have not, until recently, been viewed as means of resistance may fulfill that role under certain circumstances. The literature suggests that these resources, rather than unions, are the institutions needed for collective action.

Social and kin networks, dominated and directed by women, make day-to-day survival possible (Stack 1974) and "familize" the workplace (Lamphere 1984; Katz and Kemnitzer 1984), but they may also be the basis for collective activism (Stack 1996; Sacks 1988). Black women in particular have historically drawn upon informal networks and used them to create mutual aid societies, collective survival strategies, and labor associations (Terborg-Penn 1985). Prejudice in unions may have served to reinforce the tendency of black women to rely on these more traditional means of aid and protest. As a result, black women's networks remain an important resource. For example, Sacks (1988) describes how black female ward secretaries in a hospital in the U.S. South were able to mobilize social networks in the absence of a union in order to attain raises and certification of newly acquired data-entry skills. Stack (1996) describes how black women returning to "persistent poverty counties" in rural North Carolina were able to use networks and organizing skills to set up federally funded day care centers, simultaneously providing working women with inexpensive day care and jobs in a community with few opportunities.

COLLECTIVE ACTION IN MAYCOMB'S FUTURE?

Working-class women in Maycomb make use of social and kin networks to redistribute goods, services, and information, as described above. Moreover, young people increasingly have college educations, and some displaced workers are taking classes at the community college in state retraining programs. A few local activists in the black community developed organizing skills by participating in the civil rights movement and a now-defunct collective cash-cropping program. The resources for funding another such program, or one like that described by Stack, are certainly present in the black working-class community most severely affected by the closing of the sewing plant.

The incentive that could prompt these women into action may be right around the corner. Nash (1994:24) has suggested that "it is not only when exploitation in the workplace is most severe but rather when subsistence strategies are threatened that people move into protest actions." Workers who were laid off in March 1997 were eligible for unemployment insurance and state programs designed for worker retraining; those benefits, however, ran out in March 1998. The community offers few opportunities, especially for women, to replace the average sewing machine operator's salary of approximately $15,000 per year. In fact, the unemployment rate in Maycomb County before 1994 (i.e., before the closing announcement) was 11 percent, as compared with a national rate of only 5 percent, and has since climbed as high as 16 percent. For households where women were major income earners and often the only source of health care benefits for their families, the impending loss of governmental support may constitute a final threat to their subsistence that prompts them into collective action.

NOTES

1. The names of the town, county, company, and local newspaper are pseudonyms.

2. The following information is derived from a 1997 interview with the president of Glenwood Mills, who has since retired.

REFERENCES

Camp, S. D. 1995. *Worker Response to Plant Closings: Steelworkers in Johnstown and Youngstown.* New York: Garland Press.

di Leonardo, M. 1985. Deindustrialization as a Folk Model. *Urban Anthropology* 14:237–57.

Ginsburg, F. 1989. *Contested Lives: The Abortion Debate in an American Community.* Berkeley: University of California Press.

Hartmann, H. 1981. The Unhappy Marriage of Marxism and Feminism: Towards a More Progressive Union. In *Women and Revolution,* ed. L. Sargent, pp. 35–50. Boston: South End Press.

Hathaway, D. A. 1993. *Can Workers Have a Voice? The Politics of Deindustrialization in Pittsburgh.* University Park: Pennsylvania State University Press.

Katz, N., and D. S. Kemnitzer. 1984. Women and Work in Silicon Valley: Options and Futures. In *My Troubles Are Going to Have Trouble with Me: The Everyday Trials and Triumphs of Women Workers,* ed. K. B. Sacks and D. Remy, pp. 105–16. New Brunswick, N.J.: Rutgers University Press.

Lamphere, L. 1984. On the Shop Floor: Multi-Ethnic Unity against the Conglomerate. In *My Troubles Are Going to Have Trouble with Me: The Everyday Trials and Triumphs of Women Workers,* ed. K. B. Sacks and D. Remy, pp. 78–92. New Brunswick, N.J.: Rutgers University Press.

Nash, J. 1989. *From Tank Town to High Tech.* Albany: State University of New York Press.

———. 1994. Global Integration and Subsistence Insecurity. *American Anthropologist* 96(1):7–30.

Newman, K. S. 1988. *Falling from Grace: The Experience of Downward Mobility in the American Middle Class.* New York: Free Press.

Pappas, G. 1989. *The Magic City: Unemployment in a Working-Class Community.* Ithaca, N.Y.: Cornell University Press.

Pappas, J. L., and M. Hirschey. 1990. *Managerial Economics.* Chicago: Dryden Press.

Sacks, K. B. 1988. *Caring by the Hour: Women, Work, and Organizing at Duke Medical Center.* Urbana: University of Illinois Press.

Silverman, S. 1975. The Life Crisis as a Clue to Social Function. In *Toward an Anthropology of Women,* ed. R. Rapp, pp. 309–21. New York: Monthly Review Press.

Stack, C. 1974. *All Our Kin: Strategies for Survival in a Black Community.* New York: Harper and Row.

———. 1996. *Call to Home: African Americans Reclaim the Rural South.* New York: Basic Books.

Terborg-Penn, R. 1985. Survival Strategies among African American Women Workers: A Continuing Process. In *Women, Work, and Protest: A Century of U.S. Women's Labor History,* ed. R. Milkman, pp. 139–55. New York: Routledge.

Worsley, P. 1984. *The Three Worlds: Culture and World Development.* Chicago: University of Chicago Press.

The Periphery in the Center: The View from Public Housing in Memphis

David T. Spangler

Large metropolitan areas in the United States have experienced significant structural changes in the past three decades. Much of the traditional industrial base has moved either offshore or outside the beltway, and it has undergone considerable restructuring and downsizing. Workers with marketable skills and education have followed industry to the suburbs, but individuals without the requisite human capital have been left behind to adjust to diminishing resources and declining public services. The public sector was expanded briefly in the late 1960s and 1970s to compensate for some of the lost employment. Initiatives in housing, education, and health care were funded with federal dollars in order to create a source of alternative employment and social mobility for many workers and their families inside the beltway. The political climate since that time has favored cutting taxes to make America competitive in the global economy, and as a result many of the public sector employment programs have been dismantled. Moreover, new welfare reform policies, as set forth by the federal government and implemented by the individual states, aim to end reform as we know it, a further threat to the existing economic base. Families and communities in these declining inner-city neighborhoods have been forced to adapt to a shrinking resource base. Lack of opportunity and increased joblessness in the 1990s have marginalized these populations further than ever. Higher levels of violence, alcohol/drug problems, and other expressions of social unrest are common. Social scientists such as William J. Wilson (1987), Philippe Bourgois (1995), and others have documented the impact of these problems, which fall with particular severity on neighborhoods populated mainly by members of racial minority groups. While similar trends can be observed in the inner-city neighborhoods of Memphis, there is also innovation and adaptation. This paper will describe residents in the Mosby public housing development in Memphis where this author had lived for eighteen months at the time of this writing. Data presented here derive from participant observation and open-ended interviews with Mosby residents and people from the surrounding neighborhood.

Memphis was second only to New York City in building public housing. Mosby Homes was one of the first two public housing developments in Memphis. Both were built in 1937 during the New Deal, which provided funding to the South to assuage rural poverty and urban squalor in the wake of the Great Depression. Mosby was built for black residents, and the other project was for whites. Both developments displaced slums and, in that sense, should also be considered urban renewal projects. Both developments were built near downtown, although Mosby is two miles east of the originally white project and the nearby business district and lies just outside the area considered the eastern suburbs in 1937. The slum it replaced was called Queen Bee Bottoms, and the tract of land it occupies, a "bayou," was adjacent to an affluent white neighborhood called Scotland. According to the Memphis Housing Authority's (MHA) 1959 annual report, "There were exactly 57 bathtubs for 550 families before the old shacks on stilts which straddled the bayou gave way to [Mosby Homes] for negroes." All that remains of Scotland is a beautiful stone church as its symbolic landmark, and the "eastern suburbs" now extend more than thirty miles from downtown.

The Mosby buildings are a mix of one- and two-story brick and concrete structures that reflect the "international style" of architecture. Each building contains from six to eighteen apartments, ranging from one-room efficiencies to three bedrooms. The overall ambiance reflects the conservative attitudes of the era in which the project was developed. The buildings sit relatively close to each other and to the streets. The units are small, simple, stark, and serviceable; residents refer to them as "houses."

Located on the bluffs of the Mississippi River, Memphis was, and is, the center of commerce for the Mid–South Delta region. Cotton was the primary commodity traded, although there has also been trade in beans and rice. These crops were planted and picked first by slaves, then by sharecroppers, and finally by machines. Mosby is located on an east-west thoroughfare that is a major artery linking downtown to the eastern suburbs and is a long walk from downtown, the medical district, and several affluent neighborhoods, all considered suburbs in the 1930s. At that time it was also within walking distance of local manufacturing plants and the riverfront, which provided jobs for residents. The factories are now gone and the commercial riverfront, largely mechanized, has moved further south to President's Island.

The first residents of Mosby were working-class families. Many were fresh from the slums surrounding downtown that had been crowded with recent rural migrants. Many were members of former sharecropping families forced off the land as new agricultural technology, particularly tractors and cotton pickers, replaced their labor. The households, made up of one or more wage earners, extended family, and children, were a select group. One former resident remembers that people competed to get apartments; he said, "It was considered a move up." The elders remember "good times" when work was plentiful and the nascent civil rights movement of the 1950s promised that they would overcome.

Many male residents worked in the construction industry, both as skilled and unskilled laborers. Some worked for the sanitation department, picking up garbage and maintaining streets and parks. Some men also worked for local industries. Still others worked as groundskeepers, gardeners, and drivers for the affluent families living on nearby estates. Many of the women worked at nearby hospitals in the expanding medical district. Some were nurse's aides, and others worked in the cafeteria, laundry, housekeeping, and maintenance services. Some worked for local retail stores, others for local industry, and still others as domestics who cooked, cleaned, and provided child care for the affluent.

Public transportation and child care were crucial factors in making a living for households with multiple wage earners. Employment sites could be reached by bus or by walking, as autos were still considered a luxury as late as the 1950s. Kin and social networks provided cooperative child care. As one who was a resident in the 1950s put it, "We had a deep sense of community." Social interaction and cooperation were said to be the norm.

Even as the civil rights movement was yielding important political and social benefits in the 1960s, interstate highways enclosed the inner city. No longer dependent on river or rail for transportation, industry began moving its increasingly truck-oriented commerce to the suburbs, often to new industrial parks that were built by city, county, state, and federal tax dollars. As industry moved out of the city, so did the white segment of the workforce, which was able to find affordable housing in the suburbs. These changes left many African Americans in Memphis behind. Their plight came to be symbolized by the sanitation workers' strike of 1968 (Collins 1976). Protest demonstrations, marches, and finally riots resulted in a declaration of martial law, enforced by the National Guard. The murder of Dr. Martin Luther King Jr. in the midst of this strike focused national attention on the extreme socioeconomic problems of the inner city, although the publicity about the violence only served to accelerate white flight and make it possible to ignore the problems left behind. Court-ordered school desegregation in 1971 caused yet another wave of migration to the suburbs by the relatively affluent, resulting in even more isolated urban communities. Moreover, Collins and Noblet (1977) describe how many whites opted for private schools, especially those operated by religious groups, rather than send their children to desegregated public schools; as a result, de facto segregation remains in the educational system.

Public housing was desegregated in 1964 with the passage of the national Civil Rights Act, but in Memphis it soon became predominantly black, and so it has remained. While seven additional public housing developments were added from the 1940s through the 1960s, the number mushroomed in the 1970s. In just five years, thirteen public housing developments were built throughout the metropolitan area, including four high-rises for the elderly. Public housing has become a way of life for many Memphis blacks, although those who were positioned to take advantage of the social transformation brought about by the civil rights movement formed a nascent black middle class. While they still lagged behind their white counterparts, many gained secure, stable employment with growing government agencies, such as public schools, the Department of Human Services, and the Memphis Housing Authority, which manages public housing. The emergence of this black middle class meant that a community that once had been unified was now stratified by socioeconomic class. As black professionals moved to the suburbs, the inner-city neighborhoods were left without effective leadership. This segregation by class—and the resentment it provokes—has steadily increased over the past thirty years. The emergence of "two nations of black America" has been documented by Wilson (1987).

Public housing residents remain mostly black, undereducated, and lacking the skills needed to meet the challenges of changing industrial technology. They have been effectively isolated in inner-city compounds. The elusive ideal of integration did not come to pass for this group. They live in black neighborhoods, go to black schools, attend black churches, work in a predominantly black workforce, frequent businesses that cater to black customers, and socialize with other blacks *of their own class*. They interface with government agencies and related social institutions that are managed, for the most part, by members of the black middle class, many of whom were raised in the same neighborhoods, but who now live, work, worship, and play elsewhere. In this relatively isolated milieu, certain strategies originally developed to help the black community survive earlier crises have been adapted to the current social, economic, and political realities. These efforts are best understood as social networks that operate on the basis of the art of informal negotiation. As such, they function to enhance survival in a volatile, dynamic environment on the margins.

Collins (1976) has described relationships based largely on kinship that sustained many newly urban blacks while benefiting their rural kin. Those networks provided jobs, food, and a place to stay in the city, and they returned cash and commodities to the countryside. A generation later those relationships seem to have been supplanted by networks within the city. Kinship remains the organizing principle, but fictive kin relationships, similar to those described by Liebow (1967), Stack (1974), Bourgois (1995), Wilson (1987), and Edin and Lein (1995), seem to be more prevalent. These relationships, while still functional, are volatile, often oppositional, and therefore short-lived and extremely unstable.

For example, men who hang out on street corners use a practice called "ten on—ten off" when they have not seen one another for a while. One man initiates what appears to be an argument with another by being verbally challenging, loud, and threatening. This behavior is usually a public display in the midst of a crowd of other men, only some of whom may already be friends. The second man responds in kind, trading threats, challenges, and insults with the other. He "gets in his face," as the men put it. This stand-off lasts a few minutes, after which they walk away from each other, only to return and repeat the performance with even more intensity. After perhaps three such confrontations, they break apart, laughing and sometimes shaking hands, often hugging. They also begin to call each other by their street names to indicate that they are really intimate old friends. It was explained to me that this ritualized greeting assures both men that neither has changed since their last meeting and can still be trusted. At the same time, it assures those present that the stranger is trustworthy. The lack of long-term stable relations, often even with family, accentuates a generalized lack of trust, approaching paranoia.

This group has been ostracized not only by whites but also by other blacks, many of whom may be kin; socioeconomic diversity is common in black families. A negative image of inner-city ghettos has been nurtured by the media, and to be identified with "the projects" has been a source of shame. The residents' response has been to reinterpret the pejorative, so that being from "the hood" is now a positive identification. A sense of place, shared history, and experience often define a community (Mintz and Price 1976).

INFORMAL NEGOTIATION

In the context of public housing, disenfranchisement simply means that democratic processes do not exist; residents have no active voice when it comes to making decisions or implementing policies that affect the quality of their lives. In this environment, negotiated order is maintained between management and residents in almost every aspect of family, household, and social life. For example, according to MHA policy, everyone living in a particular household must have his or her name on the lease, with his or her relationship to the main leaseholder specified. Casual visitors are excepted, but even in such a case, management must be notified, and visitors are supposed to stay for just a specified period. No apartment can be rented or subleased under any circumstances.

Nonetheless there are casual visitors, housemates, children who may officially reside elsewhere, extended family members, and friends staying over who are rarely in practice included on the lease; the MHA generally looks the other way. It is understood that a "house" is under the direction of the main leaseholder, who will be held accountable if problems arise from unsanctioned household arrangements. Some households include boy/girlfriends or other roommates who "pay rent" or at least contribute to household expenses. This strategy is common and tacitly accepted by management; it has been negotiated over time by residents who refused to have their autonomy questioned in their own houses, reflecting a commonly accepted norm in society at large. A recent news article (Van Valkenburgh 1998) detailed a tragic fire that took four lives and injured six people; the story revealed that at least eleven people had been living in the MHA townhouse. After a public outcry, an MHA official stated that the leaseholder had obtained permission for all the visitors and had followed all the visitor guidelines appropriately, which is not at all likely. This principle of negotiated order applies to practically all areas of life in public housing.

White flight accelerated in the 1970s, leaving inner cities abandoned, redlined, and economically depressed. Industry and jobs moved from Memphis proper to the suburban industrial parks to the east. Major plants such as Firestone, International Harvester, and RCA closed and left many urban poor with few options. Mobility in the form of owning a private automobile became a key factor in holding a meaningful job. Day labor was long an acceptable adaptation for the economically disadvantaged, but in the 1970s temporary employment agencies began to hire more people than ever before. As more and more companies relied on such agencies as a source of unskilled labor, they proliferated and have continued to provide an alternative for the reserve labor force in public housing. Both male and female residents are hired for the "nonstandard work" that is associated with the temp agencies, although the men are more likely than the women to rely on this strategy. One man said, "That's all I know. It's all I've ever done."

Most jobs for men today are temporary and short-term, even if they are not found through a temp agency. One man has had nearly a dozen jobs during the past year, but he is presently unemployed. He is a skilled chef, but has been fired from most of his jobs, usually due to disagreements about pay, work rules, work times, and work hours, all of which were negotiated informally with his bosses. On several of these jobs, he has been paid in cash "under the table," a method preferred by many for perhaps obvious reasons.

Another resident said his last "regular job" was seven years ago with IBM. He said, "What I was called was an 'inventory control manager.' What I was was a stock boy." Since losing that job, he has "scuffled" for a living. He works some days as a temporary unskilled laborer at $4.75 per hour. In the evening he may "do favors" for a powerful person in the neighborhood. When the opportunity presents itself, he may borrow a dollar or two from someone who is "flush"; he promises to repay it tomorrow, which never comes unless the lender demands it. When all that effort fails to generate any cash, he may wash car windows at a busy intersection during rush hour.

On one occasion, this man got a full-time job at a factory that provides cardboard boxes with Styrofoam inserts for other manufacturers' products. This work is done on a contract basis, and the workers are sent home when each order is filled. On average, he worked about thirty hours during a typical week. He was paid $4.75 per hour with no benefits. He actually worked for a temp agency owned by the company, but when his labor was no longer needed he was sent home without either an official lay-off slip or unemployment benefits. The state unemployment agency holds that a worker cannot collect benefits after being laid off when working for a temp agency.

Another resident, who is a skilled tree cutter, works for a boss who furnishes the equipment, including transportation, and pays him cash, usually for three days per week. On three occasions over the past year, that negotiated agreement has failed, and he has taken a job that he refers to as "full-time" because the company pays by check and withholds taxes, even though he still works only three days per week.

A number of women work for a commercial housekeeping service, which provides transportation. Every afternoon a fifteen-passenger van takes them to clean office buildings after business hours. Some women work for dry cleaners, most of whose work is done overnight. They also work through a temp agency. It is often necessary for them to call ahead and be added to a list so that they will not arrive too late to be hired. Such an arrangement requires that they know the person at the agency who is responsible for sending the required number of workers on a given night; they must negotiate informally with that person to ensure that their names are on the list on the nights they choose to work. Many of these women, most of them mothers, must choose evening and night work so that they can attend to household duties, including getting their children off to school and being there when they get home. They sleep during the day while other household members are at work or school. Some of the women still work at the nearby hospitals, but most no longer are actually employed by the hospitals themselves. They work either through a temp agency or for a private contractor that has taken over such services as the laundry, cafeteria, or housekeeping. They therefore do not receive benefits, such as health care or sick leave. They are often understandably frustrated by the fact that they work every day in a state-of-the-art health facility where they themselves cannot be treated since Medicaid (or TennCare as the new state system is called) assigns them to a clinic elsewhere.

As noted above, mobility is now a necessity in order to access the labor market, especially since more and more jobs are now located in the suburbs. Approximately one in four public housing leaseholders owns a car (CURE 1995), but many depend on someone else for transportation beyond walking distance. Bus routes are laid out in such a way that two or three transfers may be needed to reach the suburban industrial parks, a process that can take as much as two hours one way. Buses are utilized only for relatively short trips. It is important for many, therefore, to find work nearby.

An automobile, while necessary in the new labor market, is often a liability for this group. One resident owns a car that has been in the shop for over a year. He has been unable to pay for a repair job that costs just $90. Beyond the expense of owning and operating a car, driving presents other serious risks, especially for men. Police stop a disproportionate number of black men for various reasons, often resulting in incarceration. One man lost his driver's license over ten years ago due to a simple traffic violation, for which he was jailed, while driving through an eastern suburb. Another has not had a license for more than a decade for similar reasons. The point is that in one generation many members of this group have been effectively isolated, moved into nonstandard work relations, and effectively abandoned by the primary labor market where meaningful work can be found. Lacking mobility, the Mosby residents remain a reserve labor force selected for low-wage, nonstandard work in the highly competitive service sector.

THE LEASEHOLDER IN PUBLIC HOUSING

The Mosby residents are particularly concerned about the role of the person who holds the lease on an apartment. This role has evolved over the past two decades, although it is likely to be disrupted by current welfare reform policy. Households are organized around leaseholders, the majority of whom are women. A man often stays with a woman, perhaps a girlfriend, mother, or sister, who is a leaseholder; in such a case, he will contribute to the household. This pivotal position gives women considerable power, since they can collect cash or reciprocal favors in return for rent.

For example, one woman who is a leaseholder shared her apartment with a female friend who worked nearby and often helped with child care and household chores and sometimes contributed some cash. The leaseholder also has had a mate for several years; he contributes some cash. She has an adult son who lives with her, and on occasion her son's girlfriend and children may stay for extended periods. All members of the household are expected to contribute something, as determined by the leaseholder. These arrangements are of necessity flexible and may change as individual needs change.

This particular household organization has dramatically altered relationships between men and women, especially those who stay together. Leaseholders determine who stays and who does not, as well as the conditions for staying. They also determine the cost for staying, which is negotiated on a daily basis. The women understand, perhaps more fully than most, the strengths and limitations of black male workers in today's job market. Rather than an arbitrary amount, the "rent" is negotiated according to a complex cost-benefit analysis. Leaseholders take into account the fact that work may or may not have been available on a given day, and they estimate an acceptable contribution. If work is not available, they may instead accept help with the household chores. If, on the other hand, work is available and a man does not take it, he is still expected to contribute cash. If a man comes in without cash to contribute, he may be out of the house for the night—or for good.

A man recently knocked at my door and asked to sleep on the floor for the night. He said, "My girlfriend's mad at me. Can I stay here?" It seems he had come from work and offered her five one-dollar bills. She tore them in half, threw them at him, and told him to get out. In such a case, the man may have to borrow some cash from someone in order to "buy his way in." This man called on his boss, who pays him at the end of every day, for an advance on tomorrow's wages to cover the deficit. He asked for a ride to pick up the advance and paid me for gas with three of the torn bills.

Another man described his own experience with his current mate, saying, "She would sell me for a soda pop," meaning that his value to her was only economic—and insignificant at that. This same man told me on another occasion that his woman gave him some "walking around money" because he had been treated badly by a temporary employer who failed to meet him at work time on a weekend, leaving him broke. The fact that she gave him some money for "bus fare, cigarettes, and a beer" was on the one hand a source of pride, evidence that she was satisfied with his performance and their relationship, but on the other hand, a source of frustration to him. He said, "If she has the money to give some back, I've been payin' her too much to start with."

These examples demonstrate how men are marginalized in underclass communities. When a female is the leaseholder, she is the final arbiter of who stays in her house, no matter what the man's contribution may be.

These dynamic, informal negotiations determining household organization often shape the relationships between the men and the women.[1]

As noted above, informal networks, personal relationships, and fictive kin make up the social fabric of the community. Borrowing, sharing, and mutual aid are mediated through these networks. For instance, when an item is borrowed, the borrower "owns" it and may lend it again to another. Each loan requires a reciprocal loan or equal favor, so a person can gain socially and/or materially from the use of another's property. As in credit networks, this practice enables people to expand their resources at somebody else's expense. After a community birthday party, for example, a neighbor who served as the cook kept an unused bag of charcoal that belonged to me. When others cooked out after that event, they went to him and borrowed charcoal, which he loaned in return for some of the food being cooked. When I asked him for the charcoal, it was all gone. He told me, "Well, everybody has used some of it." He did not mention that he, and not I, had gained socially and materially from that particular resource. In all fairness, I should mention that I too have been invited to eat on some of these occasions when no one owed me anything.

Opportunities to nurture these social networks take on a ritual appearance. Beer is usually shared with those who are short today but will be flush tomorrow. There is seldom enough beer to get drunk, but just enough to socialize, which includes sharing the latest news and arguing one point or another about a mutual friend or a current affair. When a group gathers, others will often join or at least stop by to "pay their respects." Someone driving by might honk the horn and wave a greeting. These groups are usually composed of men, and so special attention is paid to all the women who pass by. Women tend to gather at someone's house rather than outside on the sidewalk. Even on occasions such as cookouts or parties when both men and women are present, groups still tend to cluster by gender.

One man recently got a night job at a bakery located some distance east of Mosby. A social group meets regularly in front of his house in the evenings. The new job required him to be ready to meet his ride, a co-worker, at 7:30 P.M., which prevented him from joining his friends or drinking any beer. After just a few days, I noticed that he was back on his regular schedule of socializing every evening. When I asked about the new job, he said, "They were supposed to pick me up at 7:30 and the other night they didn't come 'til 9:30 and I didn't go. I had already been drinking and I told 'em I wasn't going. Besides, it's a long way out there." That was his last day at work. As noted above, most jobs are short-term. The social relationships that will produce the next job and the sustenance necessary to survive days without work are more important than the jobs themselves. Rational decisions are based on personal and collective experience to work or not work at a particular job on a particular day according to the relative value for survival over time. Such practices tend to support the incorrect popular perception that members of this group are lazy and avoid work in order to socialize.

CONCLUSIONS

The similarities between members of the urban working class described in the 1960s and 1970s by Liebow (1967) and Stack (1974) and the inner-city poor of 1998 mask the great change that has occurred in the larger society in those intervening decades. In fact, statistical data show that during that time the average income of the inner-city poor steadily decreased, while members of all other socioeconomic strata in the United States have gained significantly (Edin and Lein 1995). Moreover, the fastest growing economic sector in the United States today is the *black* middle class, a fact that is often used to rationalize the groundswell of support for drastic welfare reform programs, especially from the political-religious right and a few influential black conservatives.

As described above, the inner-city poor have been finding it increasingly difficult to survive. Social, political, and economic processes exert increasing pressure on this group, which has become a source of cheap labor to be called on when needed. Moreover, escalation of these processes driven by an explosion of technology explains not only the growing schism between the urban poor and the larger society but also the escalation of violent responses to those realities in America's inner cities. It is the immediacy of dynamic negotiation on a moment-by-moment basis that informs the urgency of an abandoned working class.

This segment of the population has therefore become a redundant labor force. The situation is not entirely new for the black male population, since a similar marginal status marked both sharecropping and the beginnings of black migration to urban employment. But at this point in history, the situation has become even more difficult. As Rifkin (1995:73) has suggested, this group may now be described as a "permanent underclass." During earlier times of economic hardship, there was always another job waiting. Those jobs may have been difficult, dangerous, and low-paying, but they were still available. Today, however, this population can hope for little beyond dead-end temporary or part-time service industry jobs. There is little hope of making a living wage with normal benefits, much less attaining the "American dream." In the absence of hope, energies are directed to surviving one day at a time, rather than living a quality life with dignity and meaning.

Wood (1998:42) argues that capitalism, unable to increase its production and therefore its profits, is simply redistributing wealth in favor of those who are already wealthy, a strategy that takes away resources once earmarked for the poor. She goes beyond Rifkin's thesis and states, "Changes in the patterns of labor toward growing insecurity may have more to do with this process of redistribution than with an absolute decline in the need for labor. The ability of capitalism to absorb a growing reserve army of labor is at least in question." Speaking of pressures that escalate to violent confrontations by ethnic minorities in so-called Third World countries, Tambiah (1994:438, emphasis added) notes, "One such strain occurs when the importation of a category of manufactured goods from the West threatens a local craft or *makes a local service group redundant and dispensable.*"

Current state welfare reform programs emphasize placing recipients in jobs. "Families First of Tennessee" is by definition a "work program" that promises various services that will prepare people for meaningful jobs. My questions are simple: Where? Doing what? And paying how much? The number of workers forced to take low-wage jobs in an already overcrowded secondary labor market can only increase when more people are forced off the welfare rolls; that increase will lead to further competition for jobs, driving wages down and resulting in greater profits for business.

Research has shown that the average Families First participant earns $5.38 per hour and works between thirty and thirty-five hours per week. Many jobs last only ninety days before a second job must be found (CBER/CMS 1997). As Edin and Lein (1995) demonstrate, welfare reform for most will result in families moving off welfare to become the "working poor." Welfare reform programs have earmarked all the resources for women and children, which will certainly further marginalize men and increase pressure on households, resulting in even more violence, social disruption, and isolation. When asked about resources for men in the Families First program, one Mosby resident responded, "What the men get is incarceration for back child support."

It is apparent in my neighborhood that upward redistribution of wealth in this society continues. Welfare reform in its current form reduces resources and curtails important adaptations in community organization. The new initiatives are supported by popular media that have been mesmerized by the objectives of free trade (globalism) and the so-called new competition without much concern for fairness or the lack of social justice for people such as the residents of Mosby Public Housing.

NOTES

1. See Liebow (1967), Kiel (1966), Whitehead (1978), Brana-Shute (1979), and Edin and Lein (1995) for more detailed discussion of "finance-romance" relationships. See Collins and Finn (1976) and Safa (1995) for insights on gender and labor issues.

REFERENCES

Bourgois, P. 1995. *In Search of Respect: Selling Crack in El Barrio.* New York: Cambridge University Press.

Brana-Shute, G. 1979. *On the Corner: Male Social Life in a Paramaribo Creole Neighborhood.* Prospect Heights, Ill.: Waveland.

Center for Business and Economic Research/Center for Manpower Studies (CBER/CMS). 1997. *Report to the Tennessee Department of Human Services.* Memphis: University of Memphis.

Center for Urban Research and Extension (CURE). 1995. *Hurt Village HOPE VI Revitalization Plan.* Memphis: University of Memphis.

Collins, T. W. 1976. Unionization in a Secondary Labor Market. *Human Organization* 36(2):135–41.

Collins, T. W., and C. S. Finn. 1976. Mountain Women in a Changing Labor Market. *Tennessee Anthropologist* 2(1):104–11.

Collins, T. W., and G. Noblet. 1977. Order and Disruption in a Desegregated High School. *Crime and Delinquency* 36:277–89.

Edin, K., and L. Lein. 1995. *Making Ends Meet: A Study of Women on Welfare.* Los Angeles: Russell Sage Foundation.

Kiel, C. 1966. *Urban Blues.* Chicago: University of Chicago Press.

Liebow, E. 1967. *Tally's Corner: A Study of Negro Street Corner Men.* Boston: Little, Brown.

Memphis Housing Authority (MHA). 1959. *Annual Report.* Memphis: Memphis Housing Authority.

Mintz, S. W., and R. Price. 1976. *The Birth of African American Culture: An Anthropological Perspective.* Chicago: Beacon Press.

Rifkin, J. 1995. *The End of Work: The Decline of the Global Labor Force and the Dawn of the Post-Market Era.* New York: G. P. Putnam's Sons.

Safa, H. I. 1995. *The Myth of the Male Breadwinner: Women and Industrialization in the Caribbean.* Boulder, Colo.: Westview Press.

Stack, C. B. 1974. *All Our Kin: Strategies for Survival in a Black Community.* New York: Harper and Row.

Tambiah, S. J. 1994. The Politics of Ethnicity. In *Assessing Cultural Anthropology,* ed. R. Borofsky, pp. 430–42. New York: McGraw-Hill.

Van Valkenburgh, J. 1998. Flames in South Memphis Apartment Kill Four: Grandma Tosses Baby to Safety. *Commercial Appeal,* January 11:A1, A13.

Whitehead, T. 1978. Residence, Kinship, and Mating as Survival Strategies: A West Indian Example. *Journal of Marriage and the Family* 23:817–28.

Wilson, W. J. 1987. *The Truly Disadvantaged: The Inner City, the Underclass, and Public Policy.* Chicago: University of Chicago Press.

Wood, E. M. 1998. Class Compacts, the Welfare State, and Epochal Shifts. *Monthly Review* 49(8):24–43.

Challenging Market-Based Health Care Reforms in New York City: Community Health Centers, Public Hospitals, and Grassroots Advocates

Sara R. Collins

The most severe problems of the U.S. health care system—lack of or inadequate health insurance, limited access to health care, underfunded clinics and hospitals, and high patient-to-physician ratios—continue to be concentrated in low-income communities. These communities are in a sense defined by poor health in that their residents generally have above-average rates of low birthweight and infant mortality and higher rates of morbidity and mortality from hypertension, heart disease, diabetes, and various forms of cancer than are found among residents of wealthier communities. These health problems have been found to have an inter-dependent relationship with low income and unemployment, poor and unstable housing, poor nutrition, and environmental pollution (Ford 1995; Hughes and Simpson 1995; Lynch 1995).

Epidemiological research shows a relationship between low-income communities and poor health, but the attention of current health policy analysts, health services researchers, and the health care providers has focused on improving health outcomes at the individual level (Black and Roos 1998). This trend has coincided with the rise of managed care and the emphasis on treating health care as a commodity that is bought and sold on an open market. Consumers and their employers are assumed, by proponents of this model, to be fully informed about price and outcome measures offered by health plans and providers, so that they can make informed decisions about where to purchase health care.

This model was advocated by health economists beginning in the early 1970s, and it has found a receptive audience among market-oriented policymakers at the federal and state levels. It is, nonetheless, a departure from past models of public health that have viewed health care as a social good or as a necessity like food or clothing (Melhado 1998). Academics and health policy advocates in the 1960s not only prescribed health insurance for the poor and elderly as a way of improving health care but also called for the planning of health systems to ensure equitable distribution of health care resources. The most significant results of this approach were the Medicare and Medicaid programs and the development of community health centers in 1965 (Melhado 1998; Morone 1990; Shonick 1995).[1] The Medicaid and Medicare programs were individually focused health policy changes, but the health centers were community-based institutions designed to improve access to health care and redistribute resources to low-income areas. Moreover, the program emphasized, with varying degrees of commitment, the involvement of community members in the governance of the institutions (Morone 1990:273; Schlesinger 1997). The community health centers survive to this day, albeit on a far smaller scale than the program's designers envisioned.

In some cities, including New York, the community health center program nurtured a highly politicized coalition of community health centers, public hospital community advisory boards, health care worker unions, and grassroots political activists, all of whom have concentrated on securing and maintaining health care resources for low-income communities. In New York City (NYC), these coalitions have involved community residents themselves in the governance of health centers and advisory boards and in lobbying efforts. Coalition efforts in the 1990s have focused nearly exclusively on resisting local, state, and federal plans to transfer responsibility for providing health care to the private sector.

I will demonstrate how market-based reforms came to dominate health policy in the United States, which has largely abandoned the social welfare focus of health policy that was prevalent in the 1960s. I will trace the development of the community health center program and the NYC public hospital system and show how these institutions created a core constituency committed to the ideal of community-focused health care. I go on to examine how the coalitions described above accurately perceived that market-based reforms had the potential to remove health resources, such as public hospitals and community health centers, from low-income communities, where they would be replaced by institutions managed from distant corporate offices, effectively sounding the death knell of the community-focused health care model. The networks' minor successes in resisting or influencing the design of these reforms is discussed. Finally, I propose that similar networks be encouraged to flourish in other cities, and I discuss ways in which policymakers might utilize this important resource in future health system reform.

POPULATION-BASED DIFFERENCES IN HEALTH STATUS

Epidemiological research has consistently shown a relationship between low income and poor health. Roos and Mustard (1997) analyze Canadian data to demonstrate that death rates from all chronic diseases among the poorest 20 percent of citizens are 70 percent higher than those in the highest income quintile. Death rates from ischemic heart disease are 70 percent higher among the poorest 20 percent of citizens than in the highest income group, 120 percent higher for diabetes, and 240 percent higher for all deaths before age 75 ("premature mortality rate"). Wilkinson (1996) reports that countries with the highest rates of income inequality have the lowest life expectancies. In a similar vein, Kennedy, Kawachi, and Prothrow-Stith (1996) report that individuals living in U.S. states with the highest income inequality have the poorest conditions of (self-reported) health. Polednak (1996) demonstrates that black infant mortality is highest in the most segregated neighborhoods in a sample of large U.S. cities.

In New York City, unadjusted vital statistics reveal a similar pattern. Seventy percent of live births in 1995 in an area of the city that includes higher-income neighborhoods (Kips Bay–Yorkville) had no known maternal risk factors[2] for low birthweight and infant mortality (NYCDH 1995). In contrast, just 13 percent of births in Central Harlem in that year had no known maternal risk factors. Low birthweight and infant mortality are symptomatic of these risk factors and other manifestations of poverty such as poor housing, inadequate nutrition, and stress (Shiono et al. 1997). Central Harlem, East Harlem, Mott Haven, and Bedford-Stuyvesant (all low-income neighborhoods) have rates of low birthweight and infant mortality that exceed the city average.

THE RISE OF THE NEOCLASSICAL PARADIGM
IN HEALTH POLICY

Despite a vast body of evidence concerning the relationship between poverty and poor health, much of the recent clinical and health services research has focused on improving health at the provider or hospital department level, rather than at the population (or community) level (Black and Roos 1998). Studies have nonetheless found relatively minor margins for improvement in hospital outcomes. For example, Dubois and Brook (1998) estimate that 14–27 percent of hospital deaths may be preventable. Much of the attention paid to the improvement of health performance of institutions has arguably been driven by the rise of managed care and, more fundamentally, by the increasing dominance of neoclassical economics in health services research and health policy analysis. Economists in the 1970s began to see health care as a good that could potentially fit into neoclassical formulations of supply and demand. Health care was therefore either a commodity whose consumption was a function of price, income, and taste, like other economic goods, or an investment that consumers purchased in order to produce good health. The policy impetus behind this work was the need to arrest rising costs in the Medicaid and Medicare programs and to ascertain whether universal health insurance would actually increase social welfare. At the center of this research was the identification of the determinants of health care demand and the analysis of the role of co-payments and deductibles in constraining demand (Melhado 1998).

This neoclassical model of health care demand and supply, which identifies a sovereign consumer with a given set of preferences and which, by definition, does not concern itself with distributive justice, left behind two traditional models of health care used by social scientists: social conflict and social welfare models (Melhado 1998). The social conflict model regards health care as a need like food, clothing, and shelter; as such, it is essential to survival, even though the wealthy try to exclude the poor from access. The social welfare perspective views health care as a special good that society should provide to all citizens. Both models emphasize planning of health care delivery systems to meet the needs of populations. The social scientists who developed such models were generally normative in their policy prescriptions, speaking in terms of what governments and institutions *should* do to achieve certain policy outcomes. In contrast, those economists and others who used neoclassical models to study health care problems avoided advocating one policy over another; they strove simply to evaluate policy, leaving it to policymakers to decide what to do with the information (Melhado 1998). Moreover, because the neoclassical paradigm is unconcerned with equity, health policy was narrowly evaluated in terms of efficiency (Rice 1997).

The growing use of neoclassical economics in health policy evaluation coincided with the rise of a conservative, market-based orientation in public policy (Melhado 1998). Rising medical inflation, particularly in the Medicare and Medicaid programs, became the overriding obsession of U.S. health care policy beginning in the 1970s. The ever-growing share of gross national product consumed by medical care was seen by elected officials, especially state officials who were responsible for paying Medicaid costs, and by the media as occurring at the expense of consumption of other commodities. The conclusion was reached that this growth should be curtailed (Melhado 1998; Morone 1990:266). Economists Mark Pauly, Martin Feldstein, and Joseph Newhouse studied the determinants of health care demand and the effect of insurance on that demand; their conclusions institutionalized the idea that health care is a commodity whose consumption had opportunity costs like any other resource. These researchers suggested that universal health insurance would lead to a reduction in social welfare and the public provision of health, but they chose not to engage in normative discussions about what governments should do to distribute medical resources in an equitable manner; rather, they offered their evaluation to policymakers to interpret and use as they saw fit. This approach set the tone for a trend in health policy analysis in which the analyst evaluated policy proposals using neoclassical economics and discounted issues such as equity that did not fit into traditional models (Melhado 1998:250).

Private institutions also aimed to improve efficiency in health care delivery with scant regard to equity. Competition has historically been central to U.S. medical care. Nevertheless, the concern over rising costs in the 1970s and 1980s put conservatives in a position to argue for increased efficiency in health institutions via market pressures. According to Schlesinger (1987), health care facilities were increasingly perceived as commercial enterprises, rather than as institutions with a fiduciary responsibility to the community in which they were located. Policymakers and health care executives, particularly third-party payers, asserted that public and nonprofit hospitals in particular needed to be better managed; the underlying implication was that they should minimize their exposure to bad debt in the form of charity care to the uninsured. In addition, the desire to create a more corporate atmosphere in health care institutions went beyond admissions policies to the governance of the institutions themselves. Hospitals were expected to form public-private partnerships so that community advisory boards would increasingly be dominated by elite interests—physicians, executives of large corporations, officers of financial institutions—rather than by community residents.

The growing for-profit emphasis in managed care also fit this point of view. Managed care emerged as an alternative to the traditional delivery of health services in the 1940s under the aegis of Kaiser Permanente. It was embraced by the political left in the 1970s, but in the 1980s it quickly grew into a market-based solution to rising health care costs. The Clinton administration constructed its complex universal insurance program around a model of a health care market dominated by competing managed care plans. The Congress defeated the Clinton plan, but the two-year debate over national health policy added momentum to the growth of managed care and the drive to find ways to decrease the rate of growth in medical costs. Managed care now commands the bulk of the private insurance market, and it has also made inroads in the public insurance programs of Medicaid and Medicare.

THE DEVELOPMENT OF COMMUNITY-CENTERED HEALTH INSTITUTIONS IN NEW YORK CITY

Neoclassical notions of efficiency have dominated health policy discourse for the past two decades, but many institutions that were created in the 1960s under dramatically different paradigms survived and embedded themselves in low-income communities in both urban and rural areas. Working at the margins of the health care industry, public hospitals and community health centers served the needs of the communities that were ignored by the policymakers and the economists who worked for them. In New York City, these institutions became linked to networks of highly politicized advocates for the poor, community advisory boards of community health centers and public hospitals, and hospital worker unions. Often working with a common set of goals, these networks became effective lobbying forces for the concerns of poor communities, particularly in the face of market-based reforms by local, state, and federal officials that threatened to weaken the community-centered model of health care that had survived since the 1960s. The following discussion traces the development of the community health centers and public hospitals in New York City and the ways in which they have created an enduring legacy of politicized health care.

Community Health Centers

The recognition that health problems were concentrated in low-income neighborhoods led to various public health initiatives in the first half of the twentieth century, such as the healthy-baby movement in the early 1900s and the establishment of health clinics in low-income neighborhoods (Schlesinger 1997; Shonick 1995). By 1930 there were over 1,500 neighborhood health centers, 80 percent of which were instituted after 1910. Most of the centers were run by private agencies and local public health departments (Shonick 1995:341).

These centers were not health clinics delivering primary medical care; rather, they were neighborhood branches of public health departments, and they emphasized personal health care education on such subjects as maternal and child health, venereal disease, and tuberculosis (Shonick 1995:341). Geiger (1984) argues that these centers were never developed with the purpose of competing with fee-for-service medicine or hospital charity wards, for they existed primarily as a means to centralize scattered social service agencies and public health activities.

It was not until the 1960s that analysts, advocates, and policymakers began to think of health institutions in low-income communities as having two related purposes: the delivery of low-cost care to the poor and uninsured, and the alleviation of unemployment and poverty, seen as the root causes of poor health in such communities (Shonick 1995; Geiger 1984). In the same year that the federal government instituted Medicaid, the federal-state health insurance program for the poor, the Johnson administration's newly formed Office of Economic Opportunity (OEO) began its own health program. Whereas Medicaid was designed to remove financial barriers to health care, the OEO envisioned a network of neighborhood health centers in rural and urban areas that would confront discrimination in medicine and the consequent shortage of physicians in economically depressed areas (Morone 1990).

But the OEO was not simply interested in delivering health care; it also saw the health centers as potentially transformational institutions linked to the local political system that would reduce unemployment and alleviate poverty (Schlesinger 1997). Geiger argues that the centers were modeled on community-based teaching health centers established by international workers in poverty-stricken areas of China, Puerto Rico, and South Africa, rather than on the early American brand of health centers. The OEO concept of neighborhood health centers envisioned communities as the central organizing principle of the health care system. Residents would be represented on the boards of the centers, which would in turn be connected to local political organizations. To further entrench them in the local community, the centers were to employ low-income minority neighborhood residents and promote citizen participation. The first health center proposed to the OEO made it clear that conventional approaches to health improvement (i.e., those dealing only with narrow definitions of health and illness) were unlikely to make major changes. It was therefore necessary to intervene in the cycle of extreme poverty, ill health, unemployment, and illiteracy by providing comprehensive health services, based on multidisciplinary community health centers, oriented toward maximum participation of each community in meeting its own health needs and in social and economic changes related to health (Geiger 1984). The OEO anticipated that the number of centers would grow to 1,000 facilities serving 25 million low-income people by 1973 (Shonick 1995).

Because the centers were a product of the Johnson administration's War on Poverty, they became a target of criticism by subsequent Republican administrations and by Congress. The dual purpose of delivering health care and alleviating poverty led to suspicion on the part of the American Medical Association and Congress that the centers were delivering inferior, high-cost health care. Such criticism led to a series of evaluations commissioned by the OEO on the quality and cost of medical care in the centers. The evaluations were generally favorable, showing that they had, in fact, performed as well or better than other ambulatory care providers, that their operating costs were comparable to those of private providers, and that they substantially reduced the use of inpatient hospital care by residents of low-income neighborhoods. Later evaluations by independent academic researchers came to similar conclusions (Shonick 1995).

The OEO community health center program was ultimately curtailed by criticism that it had not fulfilled the central tenet of the War on Poverty—the centers had neither expanded employment nor reduced poverty in low-income communities. Indeed, "the opposition from ideological opponents of the social programs encompassed by the War on Poverty was politically much more powerful and sustained than any professional fears of competition or low quality, and eventually it prevailed in diluting many of the innovative features of the OEO neighborhood health centers" (Shonick 1995:346). As a result, only several hundred centers were actually ever funded.

Public Hospitals

New York City and other large cities were the first to build public hospitals whose precursors were the "poor house" infirmaries of the nineteenth century. Public hospitals flourished in New York City in the 1930s; the share of the population eligible for care in such institutions rose to about 60 percent (Brecher and Spiezo 1995). After the Second World War, the hospitals experienced a long period of decline, during which the facilities physically deteriorated and physicians went to work in hospitals serving the middle class. The public hospitals were relying on foreign-trained physicians by the 1950s, and many were close to losing accreditation because of inadequate medical staffs. After Gouverneur Hospital lost its accreditation in 1961 and most of the medical staff at Harlem Hospital failed to pass mandatory examinations instituted that year for foreign medical graduates, the city reclassified all eighteen municipal hospitals as affiliates of medical schools (Brecher and Spiezo 1995). As a result, the public hospitals essentially became teaching hospitals; more U.S.-trained physicians were therefore attracted to them.

Under Mayor John Lindsay in the 1970s, the hospitals came under the governance of a state-chartered public benefit corporation known as the Health and Hospitals Corporation (HHC). It still operates them even though the facilities are owned by the city, which also continues to have responsibility for capital improvements. The HHC collects all third-party payments and receives a lump-sum payment from the city tax levy. It has sixteen board members, most of whom are appointed by the mayor (Brecher and Spiezo 1995).

Each hospital also has a community advisory board that in theory represents community interests. In practice, none of the boards has had much direct impact on the operation of the hospitals, although several of them have influenced the political process through grassroots health advocacy networks. Organizations such as the Campaign to Save Our Public Hospitals and the Commission on the Public's Health System have connected the advisory boards to broader health care lobbying efforts on behalf of low-income communities.

The AIDS epidemic, the resurgence of tuberculosis, and an increase in the demand for psychiatric inpatient care (which was, in part, related to the crack cocaine epidemic) all contributed to an increase in inpatient care admissions, length of stay, and occupancy rates in the late 1980s and early 1990s. As a result, the system became overcrowded; between 1989 and 1992 five of the eleven hospitals failed to win accreditation. Lincoln Hospital in the Bronx experienced the most severe crisis, losing its accreditation for two years (Brecher and Spiezo 1995). In his 1993 mayoral campaign, Republican Rudolph Giuliani pledged to privatize city hospitals, and he began carrying through on that pledge the following year.

CHALLENGING THE FREE MARKET: POLITICAL ACTIVISM AND THE LEGACY OF THE COMMUNITY-CENTERED HEALTH MODEL

Mayor Giuliani inherited a large HHC budget deficit. Refusing to allocate city revenues to fund the deficit, the mayor instead used layoffs and attrition to reduce the HHC workforce by nearly 1,300 positions. The mayor reduced the city tax levy for the hospitals by $150 million in 1995 (Brecher and Spiezo 1995), and he announced that he would sell three public acute care hospitals (Coney Island Hospital, Elmhurst Hospital Center, and Queens Hospital). The number of beds (1,240, or about 21 percent of the HHC total) to be lost was in line with what analysts perceived as excess capacity in the system (Brecher and Spiezo 1995), but the selection of the hospitals for sale appeared to be largely whimsical and motivated by only a vague goal of meeting the demand of today's competitive health care market through privatization. The underlying threat was that this ailing bureaucracy was doomed to fail in the face of competition and that public hospitals and clinics would surely close without privatization. A form of public/private partnership would increase the capital and managed care expertise available in the system (NYCHHC 1996).

Privatization of the Public Hospitals

The Giuliani administration negotiated in 1996 a ninety-nine year sublease of Coney Island Hospital to Primary Health Systems–New York (PHS–NY), a little-known Pennsylvania-based corporation with no previous experience running a hospital the size of Coney Island. Despite three outstanding lawsuits and a significant public outcry against the plan, the city required the HHC board of directors to vote on the sublease with only three days' notice. The HHC called a special board meeting on November 8 at 8:00 A.M.

The HHC board of directors' meetings are open to the public, and by 7:00 A.M. thirty or forty protestors were lined up outside waiting to get into the hearing. The group was made up of hospital community advisory board members from the area around Coney Island in Brooklyn, unionized hospital workers, and advocates from the Campaign to Save Our Public Hospitals and the Commission on the Public's Health System. Once inside, the group was noisy and the hearing room was chaotic. Maria Mitchell, who chaired the HHC at that time and who led the privatization effort, attempted to assert control over the meeting so that the vote could be held on the sublease. By that time, the room was packed with observers, protesters, reporters, and TV cameras.

Each of the thirteen board members present was allowed to voice an opinion on the sublease. David Jones, who is black, directs the nonprofit Community Service Society. He was the most outspoken contributor to the debate, arguing that the rush to hold a vote had damaged the public trust. There was a sense that a deal had been cut without public approval. During his comments, there was considerable shouting in the room from his supporters. Mitchell, who is white, responded, "Mr. Jones, can you please control your public?" A protester in the room shouted back, "This is *your* public, Maria. We may not look like you, but we are your public." Jones continued: "This is an ill-advised lease. Private hospitals [in the past] did not serve the minority population well. There was a lack of recognition [at private hospitals] for what is involved for care of minorities and poor people and people of color. [This lease] is racism! I remember the abuses of the past. Private hospitals have not shown a commitment to the poor, and this is why the government has intervened to protect the poor."[3]

The vote was 10 to 3 in favor of the sublease. Several groups subsequently filed lawsuits challenging the legality of the decision, including a coalition of community organizations and advocates. The State Supreme Court ruled in January 1997 in favor of the plaintiffs in the city council's lawsuit against the mayor. The plaintiffs had argued that the mayor must first ask the city council for approval of the sale and put the proposed deal through the city's land use review process. Justice Herbert Posner agreed with the city council's argument and added that the state

law that created HHC did not give it permission to sell or lease municipal hospitals. The decision is currently under appeal. The binding contract signed with PHS in May 1997 demonstrates the Giuliani administration's determination to move forward. The mayor suspended plans
to privatize two other hospitals during the 1997 election year, and most
policy analysts anticipate that the hospitals will be allowed to bleed to
death rather than be overtly sold off. Giuliani's larger political ambi-
tions in a state with term limits have led him to try to establish himself as
a friend of markets and a foe of big government. Giuliani fired 1,000
city hospital workers in the spring of 1998, and he would have replaced
them with participants in Workfare (the NYC welfare-to-work program)
if not for a threatened suit by Local 37, the public hospital employee
union. Lawrence Brown of the Columbia University School of Public
Health told me in an interview in 1996, "I don't think the system will
vanish, but Giuliani may starve it down to a point where it cannot be
defended anymore."

Medicaid Managed Care

One of the most fundamental assumptions of neoclassical consumer demand theory is that consumers know what is best for them and have
sufficient information and the wherewithal to make decisions that are in
their own best interests (Rice 1997). This basic assumption is the basis
of the competitive markets and is the crux of models of competing managed care plans. In these models, consumers choose health plans that
offer care that is high in quality and delivered in a cost-effective way.
Consumers will shop for health care armed with perfect information
about plans that will compete for their business until only the best plans
survive. This logic was the basis for the Clinton health care reform plan
of 1994, and it is the theory that partially supports the Medicaid managed care waiver program through the federal Health Care Financing
Administration (HCFA). Also known as Section 1115 (Research and
Demonstration Waivers), Medicaid managed care waivers allow states
to require Medicaid beneficiaries to enroll in managed care plans. States
pay the plans at a capitated (per person) rate and monitor their operations with varying degrees of rigor. There are currently fourteen waivers
in operation in various parts of the country, each of which has its own
particular design. The goal of the program is to manage the care of Med-

icaid beneficiaries with an emphasis on preventive care and the avoidance of costly use of inpatient and emergency room services.

It took New York State nearly three years to gain HCFA approval for its mandatory Medicaid managed care plan, even though many beneficiaries had already voluntarily enrolled. The state operated a small mandatory Medicaid managed care demonstration program in southwest Brooklyn. Much of the delay can be attributed to the activities of a New York City–based coalition of community-based organizations, including community health centers, advocacy organizations, community advisory boards of public hospitals, and local Democratic elected officials. Community-based networks gained the ear of a sympathetic federal government even in the context of newly elected Republican state and city governments; a powerful and much maligned Republican senator, Alphonse D'Amato, who was in large part responsible for the Republican gubernatorial victory; and a skeptical Clinton administration that included Donna Shalala, a former New Yorker, as Secretary of Health and Human Services. These networks formed the New York City Medicaid Managed Care Task Force, whose steering committee was made up of representatives of health care advocacy organizations, including the Community Service Society, the Gay Men's Health Crisis, the Legal Aid Society, the Children's Defense Fund, and the Commission on the Public's Health System. The task force included representatives from community health centers, health care worker unions, hospitals, community advisory boards of public hospitals, universities and other research organizations, foundations, local government offices, and advocates for the disabled, homeless, mentally ill, children, the elderly, and people with AIDS. Highly energetic and politically savvy in its organizing and lobbying activities, the task force in a three-year period delayed the passage of the waiver as it was initially designed and had some impact on the design of the waiver that was ultimately approved. According to Lawrence Brown, the strategy of the advocates was to lobby Washington rather than Albany or New York City. Their primary interest was to have the waiver include provisions to protect patients from abuses. Brown characterized the NYC advocates as "more powerfully organized, more inflamed, more politically adroit" than those elsewhere in the country, and they set about the task of stopping *mandatory* managed care. They were particularly effective in their threats to litigate under the terms of the Americans with Disabilities Act.

The task force opposed the waiver program mainly because its members believed that the rights of Medicaid beneficiaries would be weakened by requiring them to enroll in managed care plans without the option to remain in fee-for-service care. Moreover, the task force protested the fact that the state and federal governments were in essence handing over the Medicaid program to the private sector, thereby raising the possibility that imperfect oversight by government agencies would provide the opportunity for plans to abuse patients' rights, including the denial of necessary care. The task force also argued that managed care, both in concept and in application, was immensely complex, and if government agencies did not sufficiently educate beneficiaries about the waiver program, those beneficiaries might select plans based on less than perfect information and, once enrolled, have difficulty understanding the rules. Finally, low per-patient reimbursement rates and a potential loss of Medicaid patients to other providers threatened the viability of community health centers and public hospitals that had been operating in poor neighborhoods for years and had been serving nonpaying or uninsured patients as well as Medicaid patients (Collins 1997).

The program, which was named the Partnership Plan, was approved by HCFA in July 1997. The task force was nonetheless able to insert language into the terms and conditions of the waiver that addressed some of their major concerns. For example, the plan has a detailed complaint and grievance procedure available to beneficiaries and their advocates. There is substantive language about the inadequate provision of information through multilingual education and outreach, and the potential for marketing abuse was somewhat alleviated by enlisting a third-party enrollment broker. In addition, the program urges managed care plans to contract with community health centers and other providers that had years of experience treating a low-income, culturally diverse population and that offered substantial nonclinical support services. The program, however, does not require that managed care plans contract with community-based providers, and it did not concern itself with the problems of financing care for the uninsured. While HCFA recognized that mandatory managed care would inhibit the ability of community-based providers to finance charity care, one federal official speaking at a public hearing on the waiver said that since this was a Medicaid program, HCFA's primary concern was Medicaid beneficiaries.[4]

Despite protective language, however, glaring weaknesses in the program emerged that threatened not only to doom the program itself to mediocrity but to erode the community-based model of primary care that community alliances had worked to establish over several decades. What remained intact, however, was the strength of the community-based coalition that forcefully and relentlessly brought these weaknesses to the attention of local, state, and federal officials and that took over jobs that these government entities failed to do themselves.

A year after the approval of the Partnership Plan, the United Hospital Fund sponsored a conference in New York City on the implementation of mandatory Medicaid managed care. An official from the New York City Department of Health told the conferees that the consumer played a central role in the effective functioning of the plan and in monitoring the plan for abuse. With Medicaid managed care, he said, "We are enabling consumers to make choices. These consumers are fully informed consumers, well educated consumers, and we intend to ensure that they have the necessary tools to control their own destiny. . . . [They] are best able to tell us what is wrong with the program."[5]

Another speaker at that conference was Chris Molnar, director of the Medicaid Managed Care Education Project at the nonprofit Community Service Society; she also chaired the Task Force on Medicaid Managed Care. She said that the city, state, and federal governments had not provided consumers with adequate information and education about the program, and she noted examples of misinformation provided by city-employed social workers which indicated that the city had not properly trained its own employees. Molnar said, "We are asking a lot of Medicaid beneficiaries to understand the concept of managed care and select a plan out of seventeen competing plans . . . but there has not been a concerted information and education effort citywide." As a result, she said, "There is deep cynicism in communities with regard to the managed care program."[6]

New York City has failed to inform its own employees and the consumers that it intended to rely on both to create competition in the Medicaid program and act as whistle-blowers when their rights were abused by the health plans. As a result, the Community Service Society and other advocates picked up the burden of educating enrollees. Molnar's education project involved group training sessions all over the city, as well as data collection and research. She had been invited to speak at numerous conferences on the subject, and she received funding to expand her project to include beneficiaries in Philadelphia. Despite the fact that advocates had opposed mandatory managed care, they emerged as the most crucial element in the success of the program. The city and state had fought the advocates and community-based providers during the development of the program, but once they gained approval from HCFA, they seemed uninterested in providing the resources to make the program a success. The advocacy networks, on the other hand, were the ones who picked up the slack.

The cynicism of the city and the state also extended to the providers, or the supply side of the model. The goal of the program was to change the way in which people sought out health care and to move the system toward preventive care. Nevertheless, the government did not require that managed care plans contract with community health centers that had been providing preventive care to low-income communities for years. Moreover, when the state was successful in winning $1.2 billion from HCFA to help providers move to managed care models, all of the money went to hospitals rather than to community health centers and other primary care providers. In this instance the unions representing the hospital workers worked at cross-purposes to the community networks. Dennis Rivera, the head of the powerful union representing private hospital workers, sided with the Greater New York Healthcare Association, the main hospital lobbying group, to win the support of the state and the Clinton administration. The public hospitals (and New York City) had supported sharing the funds with community health centers.

An even deeper problem was the failure of the state to address the fact that community health centers and public hospitals served entire communities rather than just Medicaid beneficiaries. In order for community health centers to be designated federal health centers, they—like public hospitals—have to provide care for the uninsured. They receive some federal and state funding for uncompensated care, but most of their revenues come from Medicaid, which generally provides their only paying patients. They then use those revenues to subsidize free care. Years of cutbacks in Medicaid fees had substantially impaired that ability even before Medicaid managed care. The advent of the latter meant that there would be even less revenue available to finance care for all persons in communities, since the per-person reimbursement rates were set so low and because they stood to lose Medicaid patients who enrolled in health plans not affiliated with their centers (Collins 1993, 1997). According to Rhonda Kuttlechuck, executive director of the Primary Care Development Corp., a New York City–based nonprofit advocacy organization, "People don't come to health centers as Medicaid or non-Medicaid enrollees; they come as families, communities."[7]

The William F. Ryan Community Health Center is a case in point. Located in Manhattan, Ryan is one of the largest community health centers in the country, serving 40,000 patients annually on a $25 million budget. Over a quarter of Ryan's patients are uninsured, another quarter are underinsured, 60 percent are Latino, and 30 percent are African American. Ryan is visibly thriving—the waiting room is a blur of adults and toddlers of many cultures—but it has been pinched by rate cuts, and the center's directors have looked for ways to reduce costs. The number of uninsured patients rose to nearly 50 percent in 1996, and as a result the center increased its sliding fee schedule. In addition, Ryan's board opted to increase prescription co-payments from $2 to $5 rather than completely eliminate its $1.5 million prescription program. The board is still looking for ways to cut corners, but its options are limited in the view of Barbara Minch, the executive director, who has long operated by the philosophy that health care is a right and not a privilege. "Right now," she says, "we are seeing patients from all over the area and then some. The questions we are facing are in the realm of should we narrow it down to this neighborhood and that neighborhood."[8]

CONCLUSION

Community health institutions in poor neighborhoods in New York City have evolved over the years into sources of local political power through alliances with community advisory boards and grassroots advocacy organizations. Rooted in the social welfare models of public health, these alliances have influenced local, state, and federal officials and health agencies in the allocation of public health resources. Facing 1990s-style market-based health care reforms, community health networks have waged effective battles against both New York City's efforts to privatize public hospitals and the state's mandatory Medicaid managed care program. As local, state, and federal governments continue to disengage themselves from poor communities by contracting out of management of public health funds (Medicaid managed care) or by selling public health assets (public hospitals), it will become increasingly difficult for community health coalitions to ensure that the evolving health system is accountable to low-income communities.

NOTES

1. The Health Systems Agencies created by Congress in 1974 were also part of this effort.

2. The typical risk factors are no prenatal care in the first six months of pregnancy, mother unmarried, and mother under eighteen years of age (NYCDH 1995).

3. David Jones's comments were transcribed from his testimony to the HHC board of directors' meeting, November 8, 1996.

4. Briefing on the status of New York State's 1115 Medicaid Managed Care Waiver, U.S. Department of Health and Human Services, Region II Offices, New York, N.Y., August 14, 1996.

5. Comments of James L. Capoziello, chief administrative officer and deputy commissioner, Health Support Services, New York City Department of Health, delivered at United Hospital Fund Conference on Mandatory Medicaid Managed Care, July 16, 1998.

6. Comments of Chris Molnar, director of Medicaid Managed Care Education Project, Community Service Society, delivered at the United Hospital Fund Conference on Mandatory Medicaid Managed Care, July 16, 1998.

7. Comments of Rhonda Kuttlechuck, executive director, Primary Care Development Corporation, delivered at the United Hospital Fund Conference on Mandatory Medicaid Managed Care, July 16, 1998.

8. Interview with Barbara Minch, executive director, William F. Ryan Community Health Center, September 10, 1996.

REFERENCES

Black, C., and N. P. Roos. 1998. Administrative Data: Baby or Bathwater? *Medical Care* 36(1):3–5.

Brecher, C., and S. Spiezo. 1995. *Privatization and Public Hospitals: Choosing Wisely for New York.* New York: Twentieth Century Fund.

Collins, S. 1993. Desperate for Doctors: America's Poor Need More Health Care, Not Just Health Insurance. *U.S. News and World Report,* September 30:30.

——. 1997. *Who Are New York City's Uninsured?* New York: Office of the Public Advocate for the City of New York.

Dubois, R. W., and R. H. Brook. 1998. Preventable Deaths: Who, How Often, and Why? *Annals of Internal Medicine* 109:582.

Ford, R. P. 1995. Higher Rates of SIDS Persist in Low-Income Groups. *Journal of Pediatrics and Child Care* 31(5):408–11.

Geiger, J. 1984. Community Health Centers. In *Reforming Medicine: Lessons of the Last Quarter Century,* ed. V. Sidel and R. Sidel, pp. 9–32. New York: Pantheon.

Hughes, D., and L. Simpson. 1995. The Role of Social Change in Preventing Low Birth Weight. *The Future of Children* 5(1):87.

Kennedy, B. P., I. Kawachi, and D. Prothrow-Stith. 1996. Income Distribution and Mortality: Cross-Sectional Ecological Study of the Robin Hood Index in the United States. *British Medical Journal* 312:1004–7.

Lynch, J. 1995. Socioeconomic Status and Carotid Atherosclerosis. *Circulation* 92(7):1786–92.

Melhado, E. 1998. Economists, Public Provision, and the Market: Changing Values in Policy Debate. *Journal of Health Politics, Policy, and Law* 23(2):215–63.

Morone, J. 1990. *The Democratic Wish: Popular Participation and the Limits of American Government.* New York: Basic Books.

New York City Department of Health (NYCDH). 1995. *Summary of Vital Statistics, 1990–1995.* New York: Office of Vital Statistics and Epidemiology.

New York City Health and Hospitals Corporation (NYCHHC). 1996. *A Better Future for Your Family's Health.* New York: NYCHHC Office of Communications.

Polednak, A. P. 1996. Trends in U.S. Urban Black Infant Mortality, by Degrees of Residential Segregation. *American Journal of Public Health* 86(5):723–26.

Rice, T. 1997. Can Markets Give Us the Health System We Want? *Journal of Health Politics, Policy, and Law* 22(2):383–426.

Roos, N. P., and C. A. Mustard. 1997. Variation in Health and Health Care Use by Socioeconomic Status in Winnipeg, Canada: Does the System Work Well? Yes and No. *Millbank Memorial Fund Quarterly* 75(1):89–111.

Schlesinger, M. 1987. Paying the Price: Medical Care, Minorities, and the Newly Competitive Health Care System. *Millbank Memorial Fund Quarterly* 65 (suppl. 2):270–96.

———. 1997. Paradigms Lost: The Persisting Search for Community in U.S. Health Policy. *Journal of Health Politics, Policy, and Law* 22(4):937–92.

Shiono, P. H., V. A. Rauh, M. Park, S. A. Lederman, and D. Zusker. 1997. Ethnic Differences in Birthweight: The Role of Lifestyle and Other Factors. *American Journal of Public Health* 87:787–93.

Shonick, W. 1995. *Government and Health Services.* New York: Oxford University Press.

Wilkinson, R. G. 1996. *Unhealthy Societies: The Afflictions of Inequality.* London: Routledge.

Contributors

JOHN R. BORT is an associate professor at East Carolina University. His research in Central America spans the past twenty-five years. He has worked extensively with the Ngobe (Guaymi) Indians of western Pennsylvania as well as with traditional artisanal fishermen in Panama and Costa Rica.

SARA R. COLLINS is an economist and senior program officer at the New York Academy of Medicine in New York City. She has conducted research on the uninsured served by health care delivery systems in New York City and on demographic differences in the use of health care services among people with AIDS in the New Jersey Medicaid program. Her current research involves the conversion of nonprofit hospitals to for-profit ownership and the corporate consolidation of managed care.

THOMAS W. COLLINS is a professor of anthropology at the University of Memphis where he teaches courses on political economy, the anthropology of work, and community development. His research has focused on the impact of industrial change, preparation of youth for the labor market, and organizing of public sector employees. He is coauthor of *Stratification and Resegregation: The Case of Crossover High School, Memphis* and editor of *Cities in a Wider Context.* He is currently researching the impact of recent welfare reform legislation on the working poor in Memphis.

BARBARA J. GARRITY-BLAKE is a visiting assistant professor at East Carolina University. Her research interests are fisheries, environmental policy, labor history, and the South. She is author of *The Fish Factory: Work and Meaning for Black and White Fishermen of the American Menhaden Industry.* She lives in the coastal community of Gloucester with her husband and son.

MARK A. GREY is an associate professor of anthropology at the University of Northern Iowa. He specializes in small towns that experience rapid influxes of minority immigrants and refugees as a result of labor practices in the meatpacking industry. He is often called upon to assist rural midwestern communities as they address the social and economic consequences of this demographic change.

MARGARET W. KEDIA is a doctoral candidate in cultural anthropology at the University of Pittsburgh. Her experience in Malaysia includes working for two years with the U.S. Refugee Program, serving as an intern in the United Nations Development Program, and conducting dissertation research funded by grants from the Fulbright Fellowship Program and the National Science Foundation. She is currently completing her dissertation and is involved with some freelance consulting.

MARK MOBERG is a professor of anthropology at the University of South Alabama. His specializations are in political economy, the anthropology of work, and rural development, both in Central America and the United States. He has published many journal articles as well as two books: *Citrus, Strategy, and Class: The Politics of Development in Southern Belize* and *Myths of Ethnicity and Nation: Immigration, Work, and Identity in the Belizean Banana Industry.* He is currently at work on a project examining environmental politics and social movements in Mobile County, Alabama.

JAMES C. SABELLA is a professor of anthropology at the University of North Carolina at Wilmington. His research focuses on economic and social dynamics in artisanal fisheries and small-scale aquaculture in South and Central America. He has also collaborated on studies of aquaculture and the growth of Hispanic communities in southeastern North Carolina.

TARA SKIPPER is a doctoral candidate in sociocultural anthropology at Southern Methodist University. She conducted dissertation research in a town in southern Alabama, with a focus on the community's encounter with global capitalism.

DAVID T. SPANGLER earned his MA degree from the University of Memphis. He is an urban anthropologist who lives and works in Memphis. He recently completed an eighteen-month field study as a resident in a public housing project, focusing on welfare reform policy. He is currently engaged in research in the same neighborhood assessing a transitional housing program for people recently arrived in the United States via Refugee Resettlement Services.

JOHN D. WINGARD is an assistant professor of anthropology at the University of Memphis. His recent research interests have centered on the political ecology of resource management, particularly in coastal and marine fisheries. Before entering academia, he worked for several years for the federal government as an economist with the Foreign Agricultural Service and as an anthropologist for the National Marine Fisheries Service.